Marvelously at sea in swells of voluptu unravels itself faster than the narrator wake a great momentum that keeps ide .... across a shifting scape of ever-changing ocean. *Anon* draws on both senses of the word; the I that tries to tell us its story dissolves into its very telling while eternally deferring its landing. Seidenberg's command of language is astonishing, building up into great orchestral swells that carry us along in the sheer beauty of their sound—it's a tour de force of linguistic imagination.

—Cole Swensen

This is a philosophical meditation on sensation, being, and discontentment, on the ways that the "flesh is rent in twain by such a biding paragon of super fluent longings." What purpose has a "depthless whorl of poesy" to what is lost, to what is left behind? There is a music in the intriguing sonic interrogation/investigation of thought and its forms and formal restraints. To enter Seidenberg's text is to confront the impossibilities of holding all of being's and sensation's and experience's complexities in a single phrase or word or line of thought. There remains only the trace elements of experience that we are just able to sense in the linguistic constellations Seidenberg constructs. Relational possibilities are activated through a remarkable linguistic acuity. This is a tracking of thought, of the possibilities of thought across time, of the limitations of knowing, of the "integral abyss" of the self. It is a marvelous wonder. Fall in. Fall headlong in.

—Tonya Foster

On these aphoristic seas made of "nothing but words" we sail on vast lexicons of maritime lore. From Ahab's bitter conquest to Noah's weathered flood, Anon musters "the allegory out of which this repetition issues, as a dreamer stepping into the miasma of the dream...", each dense aphorism a verbiage ocean or island "describing the presence of an absence"; each imperilled mandate to divergence another "telling by revealing the perversity of the told." Seidenberg's recursive, lyrical explorations of time and narrative, knowledge and beauty, float through an archipelago of "lapidary prosody," an ever more insistent "interregnum of ellipses," part Melville, part Wittgenstein, part Kant, until the narrator's ecstatic realization—"Memory is taken back and given by the ocean...; gleaners such as you and I, are alone enjoined to make a survey of the wreckage, and fashion what remains into..." *Anon* is that survey and that fashioning, all to submerge its readers in this shimmering sea mirage, in which we luxuriate while we plumb the mysteries of the abyss.

—Susan Gervirtz, author of *Hotel ab*c

Anon

Anon

Steven Seidenberg

OMNIDAWN PUBLISHING
OAKLAND, CALIFORNIA
2022

Cover image from the series *"Rome Squares,"* by Steven Seidenberg

Cover and interior typeface: Garamond Premier Pro

Cover and interior design by Ken Keegan

Library of Congress Cataloging-in-Publication Data

Published by Omnidawn Publishing, Oakland, California
www.omnidawn.com   (510) 237-5472
10 9 8 7 6 5 4 3 2 1
ISBN: 978-1-63243-105-9

I

All the same I thought myself a less likely pauper than corpse, and approaching both with neither speed nor trepidation, dreamed the dreary languor of this medial repose a passage to the nearest port, where I might yet be freed of the compulsion to believe myself conscripted to the screed of fixed horizons. It is my way to grieve what once was mine, to beat perforce another path, when loosed from all the self-effacing credos of a fool I can again—if not at last—exude the fetid humor of this incidental gash, a glancing wound that ever bleeds from nowhere towards the real. When I promenade in lockstep with each funeral procession I encounter on my way and find in every prized and praising eulogy the giddy stimulation of solicitous reproach; when every faint distortion seems a respite from the swooning obligations of a tortured light, and no other can declaim a greater purpose than this shrift, lacking in composure the enchantment of utterance or caress, I croon the sonant gospel of extinction with a forced, anomic smile—to flow again as water spilled, and gathered to the sea...

φ

When I warble it to pigeons preening on the trail, and think myself the fairest of all murderous successions long since driven from the drink; when I press to play the vaudeville *Guignol* on that pretense of a stage and dig a shelter for a grave in quiet, painfully delectable anticipation, pleading in recumbency for the cleansing inundation only such an incidental surfeit can complete; when the terra set beneath me seems no more reliable a perch than any melting iceberg drifting low upon the waves, and each new leap towards solid ground settles as another nervous wobble lurching sideways after plumb, then I account it high time to set out upon that most inscrutable of atmospheric lineaments, shimmering and distilled, making for the coast with as much haste as possible. If they but knew it, almost every suppliant would seek the same unalterable limits, off to sail the seamless grade upon which every tangent, every pivot...

φ

So call me what you will. Some time ago—never mind how long—having emptied out my pockets to reflect the void of interest I had once again presumed to limn my enterprise on land, I thought that I would hitch my line to some haphazard freighter, indiscriminate in choice of mate or ancillary crew, and survey some small portion of the remnants of the deluge, as though to take a measure of the failure of that carnage to achieve its due. Call me foundling or free, a penance too depraved to offer, neither lineage nor birthright to repudiate or claim, this first flounce of acquaintance will not prove an easy target, and as such I implore you to stay with me through the transit, guaranteed the pleasure of some forthcoming diversion in surrendering your easement to the runoff of this rancid rill. And just as other swindlers find the flood gates of the wonder-world swung wide by the controlled conceits and undeliverable perils of some derogating code, so the prudent zeal of this crude penury of forms compels me to find entrance to a loftier derangement, following the course of any pathway through the thorns of lavish copse and threadbare thicket to a dreamed apotheosis—a feint assured as well as witnessed—in a speechifying plunder of the harbor, then the rime...

φ

Is it so surprising, really, that those whose flesh is rent in twain by such a biding paragon of superfluent longings—whose elemental character has been avulsed asunder by the discharge of this otherwise gratuitous *prognosis*—should want to cast a glance upon the land they've left behind without a seeming trace? Have they overstepped all limits by their need to cleave the depthless whorl of poesy to their forswearing heels, that they might comprehend at least their least and ownmost stranding of such mat and leaden pearls for sodden souvenirs of searches ended in a prepossessing vagrancy? They, they, they...If any third now feigns a deft presentiment of footfalls still secluded from this pallid churn of figments into prosody, or the credulous dissemblance of some middle term insists its functionary compass points assume a Stygian transparency—an equivalence of privations—as means to reach the beachfront from which every furtive mariner sets forth, then what, or rather, *who* am I to ferret out the regress thus mistaken for a torrent, to bar the gest before I've found the means to its discernment, as a game of tag where the only home is a tree stump on the far side of the ocean...

φ

Why not let that leaky tub float cautiously away from its phlegmatic harborage, image after after-image cruising vainly timewards in the name of some shrewd prowl; the pitying land would deign give succor, but in the gale that clot of rotted modicums presents an unmatched peril—with one small graze the polished keel has scattered into timbers, and all the crew compelled to trade the vigor of the shallows for a shroud of sodden loam. Thus ye glimpse the mortally intolerable measure of a reasoned meditation, where every effort issues from the bucket mind's desire to keep itself afloat upon an independent main, against the overweening press of transcendental muck to cast that dinghy back upon the ravaged shore. But as in dispossession from the land resides the highest truth, indefinite as any godly spasm from the null, so better to vanish in the storm surge of that ululating squall than to beat one's head upon the cudgel of the lee, vergeless but approaching the next verge of some unbounded shoal...

φ

Still the rumpled wavelets will rise up to taunt the plunderers of flotsam with the promise of a pitch that can't be measured or inclined, that can't be...whose *amusements*, as it were, may well be warrantless in turn, but no facile reproof can lay such claim to an attention more compelling or inclusive, driven as a dancer who can't carry off a single pirouette without a blunder, so bent on its refinement that there's no chance to rebalance before the stumbling plié. So it goes with me when my world is laid bare by the hunger to fall headlong from the crow's nest in despair, to throw myself into the maw that guarantees the scant estate of indisputability its ken; the sundering of depth from any surfacing facade, the shearing of the veil that rends the integral abyss...no evidence will abrogate the next arising outside without another surging forth to take its form and place, resigned to make my mark by skipping over once again, to draw my breath in viscous troughs hewn from the see-saw heaves, knowing that to sink would but enact another deficit, another loss...

φ

Thus when I am once again and thoroughly repulsed by the repair of carking ditches in the desiccated marl, I take the limpid lacquer of the deep to be an image of the bottomless entelechy that permeates each shining thrum perceivable in kind. There I have departed from the fickle thick of gore and skin, diffusing through the dissonance with every lapping wave of muddled skyline on the slopes of the new day, a freedom from all frittering defilements occasioned by my efforts to make tangible the topographic contours of the shore from which all similarly decorous prostrations must have already embarked. Each world is an island, accomplishing its shadowy remainder by accepting on the balance the discretion—the *necessity*, for necessity is *never* indiscreet—of a monstrous decay into its other. The flesh is sad, alas, and I have nothing but words...

φ

I will not say that by this feckless toil I have offered up a model of my acquiescent landings, nor even a heuristic plot by which some more adventurous seafarer might think to hoist a serried flag above the surging azure of this littoral excursus; I would not wear the cap and sash of victory even if I could, for the unwavering vulgarity of every torpid analogue, the regressive stupefaction of each attempt to replicate the clay by which one first attempts to replicate...The interval that interrupts the dawning valedictory—that's wedged between all claims to realization and dispatch—certifies the imitative novelty of each and every represented harborage, as though the act of naming were the method and the portent of some forthcoming attack. Likewise all compelled to put an end to such release, itself deprived of gang by a flippancy as irremediably deplorable as it is fatally full of interest, need only span the arid estuary on which the empty ship of state, lost among grasshoppers, stands in for this siren song of castaway remainders, a radial residuum at play upon the noose of the horizon. If an intellect transfixed by such crude transports can sufficiently subdue—in part by habit, in part by nature—the deficiencies under whose weight it has been stifled from the start, it is just as well that I return, for the second and last time, to the allegory out of which this repetition issues, as a dreamer stepping into the miasma of the dream, the vanishing point of every next commencement in its series...

φ

But perhaps it is enough, this incorruptible remittance, a conditional that intimates its differential obverse, which is equally to say—perhaps it's not; perhaps it never could be, and by this odd admission always has been from the start. I'm sure the affirmation must read as premature, for having somehow drifted into this digressive dotage of an anecdotal form, but that remains beside the point—as though all sides, unfolding inward, find their edge and terminus in dwindling away...The *avowal*, rather, can seem nothing but absurd—at least the method signified by this tossing off of passions can't arouse the confidence of witnesses who think themselves the arbiters of lo these many fitful and perfunctory controls. Who will swear the character of lethargy that provokes this glib indulgence, or parry the hypnotic charm that turns this dynasty of detours from its endless drift? Not I, that is, not any I at all, no matter if such one should take this limit as the sign—the *incarnation*—of a promissory hostelry or not. It simply makes no difference what justifies the placement of some otherwise anomalous phrasing, nor whether there's a reason to dissimulate the motif of this cipher of derangement, as long as it assumes a place within the general order it portends to circumscribe...

φ

Even as the presence of oxygen can be deduced by the ignition of a glowing match, so the prudent auditor of this narrative contrivance will recognize the accomplishment of my duty by the zeal I betray in returning to the point, preferring the droll rhapsody of these dissembling protestations to an imperious lucidity of absences. One might be right to think the insistence of this account a disaffection by concealment—a darkening of the window glass so that the yawn of an abyss appears to open in its frame—but it would be an error to consider that evasion as the turning out—so the *defilement*—of virtue. Every broad description of such tractable transcendence is a camouflage, each extrapolation of depth confers a contiguity of surfaces; the ostensively remedial indulgence of this circle of denials is the only sum affirmed by any truly figurative praxis—I will return, I will turn back...to what? Already the inceptive vault effuses with the redolence of coming inundations, already I await some eager heretic to tap me on the shoulder, delivered from the fall that strikes the aforementioned dancer by having failed to suffer even momentary discharge into graceless flight...

φ

When first I deign to bunk aboard I welcome as a lover every sojourn into port, presuming each new landing will provide another chance to chart the ruptures of tectonic bends across the pitching ornaments of thrusting tides and placid dirt; I believe that moving forward I might seize the solidarity of vacated rebukes and lead my foundling charges from the fellowship of empty marks, but this submissive deviance can only achieve bearing by turning back to seize the hand of some benumbed petitioner. I will beseech that foundling shade as thou no longer; I will, that is, cease all attempts to read the starry script of dust by forcing pick and sieve upon this child of the welter, as adamant and lifeless as the lid of a tomb, nor will I scrape compacted loam in search of some immutable morphology to proffer as my own, for the certainty that any thus palpated stone could only frame the outer limit of the only ever outside, ever alter. Someday soon that golem may again convene the caucus of a roiling ontogeny within its alloyed frame, but the speculation is still only what it's always been when considered from the purview of a life set on the cistern of the seas—which is no particular concern, immanent or otherwise, of mine...

φ

It may appear a recondite distinction, but that's of little consequence; every twin may represent a singular existence, but the designation intimates a generative quiddity exceeding mere position, mere resemblance. And so despite the singular asceticism by which I substitute this metered euphony for wit, the crcumstance that drives me seaward also binds me to the preservation of all possible retreats, the depredation of the land from which it firstly pressed to launch notwithstanding. If one can only make one's way to shore by the ruination of the ground traversed in the attainment of that blind advance, there will be nothing to distinguish that parched and withered island of inexorable confinements from the unrealized potential of farther banks. The empty *idée fixe* of every dropping of the anchor—which is to say the promise of the next *put in*—seeks not for lands still waiting to be charted just behind the promise of that diametric cipher, but rather for a harborage precisely where and what it is regardless of one's length of stay athwart the roiling main...

φ

Every seminal dissemblance of the telltale misadventure—that only by such enterprise can one discern the potency of what has hitherto set off towards those disdained composures—foments the seeming left-behind as always still-to-come. It makes no difference, I'll tell you now, what character of rot one finds clinging to one's coattails, as long as the onus fails to influence one's forward course. Yes, I say, the fallow trail one blazes on one's way towards the generic embarkation into proximate imperils will stipulate within its wake a ravaged panorama, as a teeming plain reduced to ash by some retreating horde. The conflagration may appeal to those who bring the torch to fecund grove and verdant meadow, but they will soon return from their retreat in search of hearth and glory on those same obliterated grounds, only to meet with the same appanage of scarcity by which their enemies were driven to abandon the campaign. What indomitable denizen thinks the safeguard of a desert worth the effort of a lazy drift to safety, let alone a near stampede...

φ

Which is to say that anyone who holds to the psychosis by which one sallies forward from the shivers of a life upon the land is no more likely to await the terminal effects of such peculiar meditations—to indulge, that is, this cataract of piecemeal importunities—than they are to comprehend them. Indeed I do not care to show...to *manifest* the indecision towards which these arch missives are most aptly seen as driven, for my reluctance to anoint the addressee with some new method to corroborate a faithless grasp. Faith can only function as a shibboleth for the faithful, and though I do not claim myself unfettered by adherence to some cull of baseless tracts, I will neither ground my practice nor my program in an infantile fable of the sort. Every poet is a positivist; if the assertion could be taken for tautology, the decipherment of this ordinal recitation would have been completed long ago...

φ

I am aware that such concerns remain at a fair distance from the agents of this travelogue, members of that ashen tribe which no wine of this world will ever warm; one may sit with the fellows, full eyes plied with empty glasses, and in not altogether unpleasant sadness admonish their attempts to foist the banderole of poesy upon so limp a pole, knowing with the certainty of countless repetitions they will fill their wells with ink again and try to raise priapic pen from barren pad to fill the barren gloam. I am, dare I say, just such a one, and so I wonder which tale is most worthy of recounting—the callow recollection of the penitent's return or the unwitting dejection of the baleful detour, taken, as it were, before one can accept it would result in a divergence from one's charted course. All metaphors aside, I would certainly forgo the practical amusements of this indolent inquiry if I could but proceed with the sort of demonstration that promises an answer to this indolent inquiry, at least that proves a path back to the sense of mode or story...

φ

One may adapt to live within some sprawling *mise-en-scene* without a hope of egress or completion, following each knotty circumbendibus accounted as a plan, or likewise stand stock still within the absent-minded haze of one's incompetent encompassment of practicums and fettles, turned about and fitted out with all the dizzying alliances required to sustain each froward fall, but the Gordian conspiracy of balance will release its churlish herald from that ganglia of promises by cutting the last step with the limpidity of water—just so this giddy clarity of termini leads me from my humbly distrait home on solid ground to follow the recalcitrant entreaties of the sailor's life. The difficulty of describing the impulse—of distinguishing the verge of such decampment that abuts its signal turn—is neither lost upon me nor entirely distinguished from my final supplication to the brine; one cannot clear a path to the departure signified by having since departed without realizing the ground itself will never be conceived as an inviolable solidity again...

φ

How this commutation of indifferent humors *happens*, I don't know; or if I knew I wouldn't say...wouldn't be *able* to say, a distinction which may reduce such knowing to the elision of its concurrently arising absence. No matter what the temper of my varying accounts—a prison-house constructed of occult enumerations and indelicate ascents—no distance will capture the disseverance of means and ends—of means from their ends and ends from their abstracted means alike—that lures all wingless teratoids to live a life more suited to a slumber in the clouds. For water takes as contraband the mottled earth, and mocks the palsied creatures tethering its depths, appearing to transform a chromosomal imposthume into a cataract of progress. So mobilize cabals of feckless brutes, flocking to the shore like wistful corpuscles, meandering to one at random, to many a coincidence of symmetry, as withered scabs congealed upon the open-wounded coast. All at once they flop to linen shrouds and shudder with the opiate recurrence of the wave, somehow more pathetic for the beaching of a lost ancestral dream, that in the clumsy tailings of causation lies a bygone world's repose...

φ

There they gaze in rapture from landings swarmed with rusty hulls and speak in whispers to themselves—how could it be, how could it be, to have so slightly missed the poet's life for thee, etc. All for a dip they bind their fortunes to the sea and gorge their ships with gold and booze and suckling pigs, devising ways to claim the vastness for a moat. From bloated cityscapes flee troops of splendor starved savants, scrambling to shackle easels for an oar and toil at some simulacrum so ponderous it seems nearly universal—a stroke of blue, a shepherd sleeps beside with no concern for flock or hunger; and just a larger brush or two, and low on the horizon azure wavelets capped with white, no land for sight or centuries to stop the flow. Therein lies not one reflection, but for sun and sky above, no features to betray the organs pulsating beneath, laid out flat upon the twilight haze as any moribund divinity. Such a dissipation may seem a poor substitute for pistol and ball, but for a consideration of still greater import—that there is nothing more loathsome than the grieving, listless simpleton who thinks such gesture in demise the only competent conveyance towards that supplicating eschaton, a surety proclaimed without an inference or deference, absent fealty or affection, as so is a most faithful lover also the least satisfying...

φ

How, then, that on the gentle rivulet some truculent Narcissus wastes away to skin and bone? Why, I ask, would ancients cleverer than most choose sipping water, harmless as a child's shadow, as means to execrate that brazen prig? Perhaps alone the threat of such consumptive approbation rests upon the meditative glance, the inward turning *all* engendered by the succoring seductions of the genial sublime. In Nature—and in water most assured the clotless blood of that long rot—one thinks oneself unbound and boundless for it, a part that won't concede the slightest portion to the whole, in which each portion must in turn abide the cruelty of the mortal scam. To me each one appears the same as any other, and around me they all throng to cant in bitter admiration, wondering with awe-inspired rage how an acumen so vast could stand so wistfully alone. I loom above their turbid skies as some placenta for the world, the discarded centerpiece of a longing that remains—both primordial and unconscious—*before* mortality. Thus I say exactly what I long to soon unfold—let them all drown in that antediluvian haze. Let them mortgage time for death, and death for yet another portrait to display, at rest before the ebb tide of a savage supplication. I care not for one or all, and by this droll transgression take an eager dousing for the practice of a saint, crying out the vocative appurtenance of primacy—Possession dispossessed me, *hic et nunc et ubique...*

φ

So, that is, *I say* I say, and saying that I say it say it I, that while I know no other way, it still may take a melancholy week or two to move upon the sea of clay a fire which, while unconsuming, sucks all evanescence from the hydrophobic firmament, declaring that an impotence of stratagems and tactics makes every dream of act a damning taunt. Perhaps the rain will fall again, a hail of bullets burning chutes into the pinking plains, but streaming through the surreptitious gully of the sewer each imbrued spate seems but another passage to the harbor. There, as arks are jettisoned to shadows, will every twiched concupiscence strip painlessly from bone and all the chortles of an academic stanza fall silent and forgotten but for one, but for just one...

φ

And so I tell the tale of a taunt, though any tub could just as surely carry its crude castaway from open seas to sight the shriveled land of truth—enchanting name!—affirming that impulsive divination only by and for the vicious rictus of an errant priest's remorse. I have always been less qualified for such endeavor, possessing neither the gifts of prophecy nor foresight, and so can only take to travels over land, avoiding by both grand and meek maneuver the most watery part. No, I cannot be a sailor or a patron of cargo; I will not be the cargo or the carrier, nor exchange the lives of mammals for the deaths of fish. In this I cannot help but share a naturalist's romance, if still denied an audience before the congress of creation; doomed as dodoes, one and all, I leave the speculating novelties of every servile Darwin and dim Pope behind...

φ

To this effect I happily forgo all declarations on the character of my longings and intents, and will in turn relate no schema for the head-lines of an idealogue; no vulgar garb or beatific foretop accompanies the pretense of this narrative vocation—that it is, that I am, *in medias res*. I cannot say exactly what it was that drew me to my end; some drab recidivism from which my fellow inmates suffer still...Inmates, yea, but only should the walls of that Bastille appear as an effluvium of vapors. I know for certain that I suffered from the drubbing of a distant reportage, and in response I took—still *do* take—a clarity of vision for my own bland cure. And which fate, that one or this, stands in for the symbol and the purpose of my plight? A distinction often enough missed, and of no great importance to such speculative man-ner and malaise; what now I think is not what I thought then, though differing in large part only by the tense. Most of all, I thought then just as I think I thought, and think now just as I thought I'd think— that a new life would await me should I take upon myself the bound-less duties of a sailor, to carry out the detriments of some tormenting power, as meaningful and fecund as a pebble on the shore...

φ

Perhaps one might adjudge the fool who speaks this devil's grove adrift within the maddest of deceits, and the addled wits thereby adduced in kinship with the mule's head whose crude likeness is in parallel advanced, a traitor to the species without sex or touch or tai-loring of scars. Perhaps I might present a simple model of this pheno-type—tail turned up the arse that likewise circumscribes the head— so that the visage of its maker might be limned on postage stamps and medals; such is the way of any limpet promise, stuck to the hull of every aggregate presentiment as though an aimless act of sabotage. But I am not inclined to frame a parable for the primer, no more an allegory to guide the glib distortions of this languorous disclosure. I have thought little enough of my account to present this introduction as a sort of firewall, that any who should make their way beyond it might pass unscathed to the blaze...

φ

And though the mixing of such metaphors may all too easily impugn the method I've employed to reach these dissipated ends, I tell you now I do not care, for the fact that it has served its purpose here and evermore—as the corselet of the figurative ligature into which this incantation gently settles as a feather to the flame. The obscurity—the *audacity*, even—of this inaugural sector is meant to satisfy no one so much as myself, and that hardly enough to make a difference—revealing, I'd like to think, the lack of any other effort to lurch forward in pursuit of some lost terminus again. I have done what I have done, it goes without saying, though saying it takes nothing from the import of the claim—the avowal, that is, that insofar as I have broached a hint at the conceit, I feel assured of pacifying no one. Could any matter otherwise...but no; considerations of the kind remain beyond the scope of such controlled and decorous solicitudes, and that, if nothing else, is all I ever have or will...or ever will again...

φ

If anyone construed as merely tantamount to what I am—to what I've *been*—were forced to stand alone on the escarpment of this germinal design, then perhaps they'd find this apologue as compelling as I do. I don't know for sure, but having realized that a more thoroughgoing analysis could do no better than prove the contrary, I forgo such projects and projections for diversionary pleasures still to come. It is my hope that anyone inclined to rail against such faltering compliance, couched in a dunce cap and wearing the mask of euphemism for a clerical disguise, will cease their humble browsing now, and waste not one more moment in pursuit of some ubiquitous verity, comforted in knowing that by covering their eyes they will not merely block the nauseus gleam that cleaves their foresight from the firmament, but in both degree and substance disappear from view...

φ

It is everything I've been, it is everything I'll be, though in my haste I may have postulated otherwise; there is nothing more compelling— nor less so in its way—than the pretext of this sunny disposition. I take little pleasure in declaring my intention to advance from the confessional and into some compulsory assurance, a daring less committed to the incapacity of the browser than any that has predisposed the predilection previous. This is not to brand myself possessed of some crude virtue, nor compare the courage with which I approach such valiant exploit with the mortally practical fortitude of one who seeks a living in despoil of the fissured tongue; rather I assemble as crusader after perils, in whom courage is a sentiment without regard to profit earned or contest won; and would that my indelicately adventitious chronicle did fail to guarantee the degradation of such fortitude, scarce would I have had the cheek to draft it. Such outright concession of the ignominious blemish—the undraped spectacle of the valor-ruined peal—is all that brings ecstasis to your prolix host, this bootlick of a supplicating churl; *a lickerous mouth moste han a lickerous tayl...*

φ

Who can say where it will lead, the bromide lode so wistfully less scavenged, as likely to make all the difference no difference—or prove it so, in any case, a peon to a sapience no more than implied. Such lustrative remorse is here avowed by explanation, though little of that purpose has been since composed, still less endured. I speak as if the substance of this abject illocution were long realized and discarded, I speak though without speaking, as a word without a name. And what childish dissimulation fashions the collusion of so many antithetical intents? What nonsensical elision has compelled me towards my chosen course, a devotee of action to the last? It matters only for the sense that only the ends only I tail are able to contrive the means to this ingenuous composure; how could it possibly seem otherwise, any end thought as an ending having satisfied the postulates that promise its provenience and dismissal by the by. It will all become clear in time, all in good time—as though any allotment of the kind could justify its differentiation from the last...

φ

I thought to go to sea, I say again, and now perhaps it's time for me to follow the agenda so immodestly laid out by that tyrannical assize. I wish I had already...that I had never come this way at all, or not before engaging a more sympathetic draft of my enthrallments; I may have done so hitherto and since erased it from the passage, I will neither confirm nor deny the possibility, imagining but one of many thematic exploits likely to engage the narc or scout still willing to continue the distractions of this fragmentary spoil. I have never taken pleasure in homage or commendation, and while a more aggressive posture might be just as welcome, I prefer to avoid this stripe of commerce altogether. That I may exercise a preference in this regard...I suppose one can have gleaned no such suspicion from what's been said...from what *I've said* I've said thus far. And I think it's just as well, for the certainty that any performative expression would be likely to estrange what little sympathy I hope to have inspired, however fatuous the sentiment may seem—or *come to* seem— before we're done. I'll admit it now, if never willingly again; I have not abandoned such a hope...

φ

I thought that I would go to sea, I always thought I would; what a toothsome figure I would cut, apparalled in such infantile dight, to heap the sheets with feral squalls, and tame the foam-capped swells... *or have*, rather, what a winsome shipmate I have been, a mercenary satisfied to make of any land traversed by foot or spike or flame the same featureless languor that follows the curve of the ocean's shallows, the contours of its pit concealed by droves of rippled seams. An altercation of swinging ballast and gusting ether has brought me to this moment—to the place where I began, that is, and will begin anew—by reference to a likeness as much allegorical as factual, struck dumb beneath the sweep of billowed sail. With neither friend nor foe to share the lone affections of acquaintanceship, I can't recall the turn from simple gaze to dauntless pillage. And absent any contract to ensure a fair allotment, I have yet to receive payment for my part in that first flight...

φ

First and last, it's as I've always been, the first aboard and last to stay the course that every harborage inveighs for the sole profit of some ludic privateer. Here the first betrays the last that will come first, here there is no first but last, having reached some last completion first before the first of any...*of all*, if any, foremost reminiscence can proceed on toward the last. Here the first that any last is is the first and only, here the last is first to think the first the last, the first the *second* last at least, for the fellowship thus heedlessly embroidered. But I can go no further...can *harbor* no less obviously gratified remorse for what has never been, or what has never been the first or last of what I've since recalled as taking place within such consecution...

φ

I can't go on, if it's not clear, though I will...*I have*, if only by asserting the unlikelihood of the claim. I stand before the precipice apprenticed to the suppliant sublimity of fathoms, and hungering to take a step upon the dried up river bed that twists the serried canyon—fearing no expedient release into that momentary scansion—I cower from the closure all the same. I would do something else...would eagerly pursue a different course, to finally conceive this introduction as some first-born reminiscence of the damned—of the *tormented*; surely I would find a more willing and able audience for this rambling dissimulation—more generally capacious for merely being *extant,* that is to say—had I taken that step forward at the advent of its finish, without a second thought to what is lost by having disavowed the misery of personhood again...

II

Another time, perhaps the next, will be my last; I must find some re-
lief, whether it comes by my own hand or not. Someday soon another
will prevail, a faith that, as unfounded as the next, requires neither
worship nor oblation to annoint its blessed...I don't know how such
diffident assents conform to these inflexible denials, nor how I'll be
compelled to meet the standards of so many who've been absent from
the start. If I could only understand this graven promenade of puzzle-
ments as my golden calf, then I suppose I'd just as blithely follow
that mute ruminant from the prison of its thicket, where the center
is the last and first, and any eager twitch towards dull-eyed solace in
transcendance would constitute the burrow of a disappeared remain-
der—or an ending, once again, and just as patently inscribed as any
other point laid out upon the circuit it corrals...

φ

As though it matters in what order one plucks the petals of a rose.
And though it might—it might matter quite a bit, as it turns out—it
does not here, for the inadequacy of the metaphor to implicate the
figure into which it has been realized and displaced—realized by its
subsequent displacement. It is of no consequence, I say again, what
nature of cosmic turbulence might have been averted by the ordering
of an otherwise undifferentiated series, if that lacework still can't un-
conceal the structure of the loom on which it's cast. But I am no such
weaver, of sails or schemes or portents; I work the long upbraided car-
pet of causation with the delicacy of mangled stumps, beating heavy
mitts upon the puerile symmetry of its seemingly reticulate design.
And though I labor with no greater skill than any other malcontent,
I differ by the cunning of the lamentation; if I could only ride the

zigzag verve of this repugnance to its antipodean conclusion, then at least I might inspire the pity of the witless, who can think a narrative worth its eccentricities only if the complexity of its obfuscating acquiescence is an effect of the scrivener's madness, and never the deportments of the browser's indolent vocation. With the traitorous joy of one who has convinced the faithful they alone can satisfy some distant, oblique prophecy, would each such one feel able to survey the declination of the sentimental cretin...

φ

And why not plead for just that sullen characterization? Why not swallow the considerable vanity that's sanctioned this prosaic causerie, that one might beckon the attentions of so many who would otherwise defy its exhortations? To this rhetorical I have no adequate response—or having it, perhaps, refuse to tell it now. I am that I am; my word against that of any interloper. If it is not enough to pose myself in wretched deference to the knights and squires of some cultural aristocracy, then so be it, I am neither better off nor worse for having skidded through some retinue of bleary-eyed inquisitors. More importantly, it has never been the obligation of the sailor to accommodate such indolent affections, as anyone beguiled by the bowsprit and the mast must surely know. Too many vital labors afflict the mariner who thinks to live another day to toil in pursuance of gratuitous concerns; concerns, I might add, that can only ever draw an audience of landlubbers. Indeed, I might as easily gaze into the depths of that grand nothingness as plummet to my end within the ethereal buoyancy of its pit, and if that is the fate I must allow myself to court with some insistence, then I can only do so now by first discounting the decorum of those who think the task quite worthless and in vain...

φ

I do not say what I will not, I cannot, an assertion as insightful as it is significant. I do not think what I cannot say, and while I'm fully capable of discerning phenomena otherwise intractably exclusive— to all at once wrap sinuous synapses around each paradox composed by cunning phraseology or blunder into void—I do not do so willingly, nor do I veer blindly from the breach. I have never tried to slip into the gibbet of some conjugal embrace, having found no other able to engorge the grappled vacuole—or hold against the withering protuberance—of my spasmodic ostentations and indelicate reliefs. I have taken to the sea in no small part to inhibit such solicitudes, and have no suitors of the kind for the etiquette of the sailor; no seaward penitent would condescend to couple with a beast contrived to frame these ill-matched outthrusts and intrusions, when so many perfumed libertines greet the next debark...

φ

And so to the adventure. If no one else will take this chance, the final and the best, to follow the lead of my indignant exposition before any commencement makes its promise of a purpose felt...for all my conversational ease I suppose I will not...I *cannot* know the difference either way. I will not share my intimate devotions with a vacancy, and so I find my most—perhaps also my *only*—agreeable bedfellow in an image of myself, ever hastening such numbness towards an arrogating nonsleep. It is all I have to tell right now, it is all I have as yet, and whereas I may return to what it seems will keep my word I will not do so for that reason—that ingratiating *covenant*—but only for the promise of some steadfast designation, at last and first the fragmentary portent of a name. It's all I ever wanted, after all is said, though never done—all that's said is never done...It functions as the discharge of some inconclusive standard, acknowledging it hasn't yet conformed to the anomalies that quicken so much other academic guesswork into scripted sum. I have made so much of so little, though I should think the claim can seem no more than hubris at this point. I should think so much more than I have, accepting the discretionary measure must await another time...another place in word and deed the same...

φ

This submission has brought me nothing but offense, if only by the migratory utterance—the pleasured speech—of some sartorial redundancy, admitting that I may have trimmed the cloth of prosody to fit against the awkward bulge or fleet invagination, but never for the purpose of a comfort *in* or turning *from* that adipose disguise. None of it can mean much now, of this I remain certain—nor will it, I assume, to any who might trail the queasy balm of this inviolate ascendancy. Not much has changed since I last reached the first by finishing the last first last, but that, too, awaits another moment, when that last first will take its rightful place as last again. I recall some sort of gathering, a recollection consonant with witnessing some portion of the scene, though whether I have ever done before what I do now I will not say—perhaps I could, but no indulgence of the claim would serve my purpose. And while this last assertion—that my purposes are better sated by another sort of ever thickening, if equally insalubrious, narrative gruel—has yet to be supported by any evidence at all...well, what of it. Patience is the hallmark of the most ingenious wit, and by this commonplace invective I forbid those who claim otherwise from continuing to bask in the gloom of my disclosures, both erstwhile and to come...

φ

I recall those vague environs with the most cringing of regrets, surrounded by that sullen ostentation of indifferent reprobates...I can't be sure by what means it has happened or I know that it has happened; it may be I have writ of their cruel scrutiny before, but the repetition does little to clarify the claim, if that's what it is—if it really is a claim, that is, concealed within some devious and world-weary attrition. I mean only what requires this distraction and reproof, even as assurances of that eventuality compel the purpose here, if any here there is, or connotes a nearing next—if any purpose here refers to any here to come. That such partage can exceed the affectation of its grounding I don't know; in any case the difference can only be taken as an evidentiary assertion when the purposes of both the whole and its constituents remain identical, or participate in the same portentous ends. There is never an inventory of distinctions in the whole that can avoid deferring to a further aggregation of its agency and portents, likewise always fashioned by a further aggregation of its agency and portents...and so on. Greatness, in the end, is a measure of the extent to which the thing thereby extolled exceeds its manifestations...

φ

It all seems quite preposterous, if this narrative repose seems quite like anything at all; and if it does, if it will...*one takes one's chances.* I hope this impassivity will cajole the affections of enough knavish admirers to ensure a reasonably sturdy redoubt, to find behind the fleshy moll that every monad circumscribes a future life without the fear of pillory or prance. And if this halting turn appears incongruous at best, I mean to remedy the plaint soon enough, to show that the disease continues to adduce its symptoms only in the one who thinks to diagnose it—who thinks the illness evidenced by the aforementioned incongruity, and not, that is, in *anyone else*...It is little enough to say—and even less to care—through what depleted method I might shepherd such intruders into place; it does not matter by what means and towards what ends I've come to play this monkey in the middle, as everything I've ever had has only been accordingly inscribed by taking on that ill-conceived and even less considered affectation. Perhaps I've set my sights on the achievement of that petty scheme alone; I plead my case and claim without contrition, as nothing but some merciless imposture could take the place of such confinement in the end...

φ

Those youthful indiscretions still excite a blush of cheek and clench of brow; I admit as much and expect no sympathy for shortcomings displayed so proudly and without remorse. Neither orphaned skiff nor coffin float could save my whetted peel, so drunk on water was I; with such allusive modesty alone I have endured this timeless bearing, which is equally to affirm I don't find a pitying and superior response anything but predictable. It's not my meaning or my mark, as if one could consider any other mote of motive more apposite than some previous or next. I say only that...while admitting well enough...I was ashamed—I *am* ashamed—of all I ever did to try my hand at the seductive glance, and yet I do not think I could have ever done differently and still have come this near—even *this* near—to the cessation of the *Histoire Extraordinaire* I've only just begun...just concluded *by beginning*, by this last dispatch alone. There is so much

I would rather do, or would have rather done, but I see no reason to engage in the rehearsal of one of many possible diversions for the sake of a performance I know will never come. Yes, I may well stand for—stand *in* for—something other than I am, but it is not *I* who stands to find it...

φ

Alas, I continue to subvert the methodology I've just begun describing—to describe *beginning*—by beginning to move on from its description, a futile preterition posed as the first line of a conclusory stanza otherwise unremarkable, or unremarked upon...Thus accepting an assumption to the world I would have proffered had I done so through some other means than this...than this is...It bears further inquiry—what a semiotics of inquiry might produce by substitution *alone*—but in the absence of such enterprise I think it prudent to advance the inadequacy of what I know I'll think again by some assuredly inadequate surveil. So much can be contained by nothing more than some suggested seriatim of replacements, it astounds me that the practice isn't more often applied to the narrative contrivances so frequently put forward as the works of literary masterminds. All this, and all this is, to advance the conditional claim that while my never quite foreseeable adventures have led to some inaugural repentance of the kind, this burgeoning against the insurmountable has brought me little else...

φ

I recall the life that pushed me seaward, when my comrades in that shabby harborage gathered round to send me off...to see me off...not a one aware of the vestigial proficiency alighting through the haze of that disparaaging directive. How could they know what great and shattering insights would soon cross my wayward perspicacity, when they themselves had wandered in that labyrinth for so long? I will not postulate the nature of their ends in relating such a brutal comity, nor the purposes inscribed by any glowering intensity; I'll do nothing to acknowledge any who has stood before me as a tyrant or a minion, nor surrender to a glandular excision better off expressed by panting. Of greater significance to the prospect here recanted as recalled—

though greater than nearly nothing may still be only that, may still be nearly nothing—is the risible comportment of those who would remain my peers on land. What parties do such scoundrels throw! A fitful saraband that soon conjoins the nervous seizure to the adventitious apoplexy, torn from blossoming penumbras and pitched into this eventide of droll acculturations. Such noxious heaving, such convoluted looming of the flesh upon the bone—there is little more to pleasured speech than...

φ

If I could have stayed, could have held my place...any place at all, within the hearts and minds of that confected troupe of reprobates— if I ever can again, as though I ever did—then history might yet be spared another dip into this standing mastery of retorts. But it is not my way, nor can I speak as though a practice of the kind has crept into the animus I follow like a scent. It is not my way; let anyone who stumbles over this confession only—and only to this berth—be assured I've found no other course. If I had, then this would not be this, here would not be this, and this here not would not be here at all. A proof without the proving, a life without the living, such chances do not seize the cinching collar of the average saint or sinner very often. That I should demonstrate something so clearly by demonstrating anything...it may prove the greatest gift afforded the dilettante still present to accept it, a more or less compulsory diversion from all just rewards...the *only* gift, if you take me at my word, a word that still can lay no claim upon the dispensation of a more auspicious verity...

φ

All such lapidary prosody finds its source and object in this barbarism only, and though the stone I cut is purple in its hue, it displays, I like to think, a certain clarity despite...*in view of* the occasional occlusion. Grandiloquence of the kind may proffer no clear purpose here—may only seem a pretense—but I can say with certainty that if I'd been considered with the lenity most commonly turned upon the harelip or the split tongue I never would have thought to carry out the missionary schema of this puzzlement by affecting the immodesty of the self-imposed exile; I am not home, I've never been, but for this beneficent dissemblance of a yarn. It's how I gather what I gather, and has been since before the slightest hint that I had gathered anything at all. Such incidental placement has revealed to me the pageant that I offer as the ever next effulgence of the *logos*—as if I will disclose that novel *nous* beneath the verdure of primordial concern. And over the whole course of my attempts to don a soutane cut and sutured to a bulwark far more genial than what I'm bound *within*, I haven't found a feature I can't forcibly adapt to any visionary silhouette by simple pull of thread or tuck of skin...

φ

Oh the serendipity of having lived through this delirium of marvels! If only any one of they had seemed or been possessed of differentiating gesture, if any one had had a name or face to mark as feature, then now I would describe the face, and muttering the name would rise to meet that ghostly standard...Somehow I have only bits and pieces of it left, a flash of flesh and grimace to account for what I can't conceive by more convincing measure. Some sight to prize as reportage indeed; I know that I was held within that ogling cabal, but I recall not one of those whose presence made it sound. As though by hate does each one seem the same as every other, for all the symbols and attractions that make manifest the quietude of sympathetic glances. In seeing there is love, in being seen alone resides the avarice of servitude...

φ

That were there one...that there were anyone at all I cannot say, but for the vague impression that for that fateful moment—that for that—I was not alone. I remember so little before...so little fixed in variance or circumstantial form, I can't evoke how I escaped from that contorted cradle. One can get only nothing from nothing, after all, a proposition of deceptive simplicity—a facile deceit—if ever there was. For that is what I was, or rather, and with similar effects—what I was not; I was not then, nor am I sure that I am now as any other is or has been. All such recollections may indeed proceed from naught—may only stand to signify the nothing that I *was*—though being it—the *it* that frames that cipher of a transcendental spark—suggests that as that nothing then I must have been a far sight more distinguished than the something I've appeared *since* then...

φ

I find myself compelled again by what has hitherto compelled me towards this hapless end, towards all that has been fixed by this indifferent automation to discern. I've had so little luck with any who would call themselves a friend, on land and sea alike, but for now I only introduce my maudlin observations to demonstrate a singular devotion to the main. So why continue to report on this defiant incongruity, only to arrive at the advancement of my own indifference to it? Why present the either/or of every daft disclosure when each instance of the choice has shown no clear effect? These investigations may inscribe the whole of what I've been, but in order to be it—to achieve such a discriminate conclusion with the certainty betokened by its signal admonition—I must have always somehow thought it otherwise...

φ

By this principle alone I have been led to recommence, to try my hand at this occulted inference anew, pressing to ignore what I've since proven. It endures as the conceit of every orphic canticle, the labor of each tortuous narration claimed prognosis; or it's one of many such conceits I will indulge upon my way towards those dissimulated termini, only unconcealed after surpassed, or superceded. What meaning could it hold for those who think themselves incapable of warding off these stalwart charms and trifling debasements, cast as though a lure into the stagnant pool of happenstance? What meaning—*I think none*. Why, then, should I attempt to cut a pathway through this muddle of concessions? A reasonable question, accepting that its asking will administer the answer, and so I leave my partisans to draw their own conclusions, by some bucolic euphony to find means within their purpose, and off to bash their heads against the wall until they burst...

φ

They tore about me, true enough, and so without a pleasure or ambition to adduce, with neither the beleaguered poise of mercy nor a supplicant's contrition to delay the scenic salvo into this ill-tempered post; how construe the measure of these petulant regrets, the inexhaustible hubris of one who is not one, expressly for the advent of so many equally innocuous doubts? What could this malfeasance mean, attributed to all at every moment and no one in particular? There is no other reason to deny such boundless hate, as none can be imagined there and then within the throes of these mute agonies, each its own demurring act of speech or speech of act...For there was not there one—not anyone—at all. There were only many there, and there there were not one that was not many, and not within another many was there any one there...there was not any one there...but there...but there...

φ

The problem of describing the presence of an absence...the absence of a presence...the difficulty of *narrating* this sequence is apparent; no metaphor will serve the purpose, and so I've searched the seas for just the sort of wakeful dream whose interruptions disappear without a seeming trace—without, that is, bequething rigid gash or mark upon that palimpsest of pleats. Even so, this concern most high has little to do with the exile I'm attempting to relay; I would like to say it did, that I thought to understand the land by taking to the sea, and the motive that's since led me to this whimsy could be as hastily dismissed as it's derived, but it is not the way it happened, I wanted *nothing* by it— by the leaving, by the taking, by the having taken leave...It may turn out I've taken to such metaphors of taking alone. It could not matter either way, to demonstrate the practice of an augury I've just begun to promise to repudiate. To promise, thus to demonstrate—I know no more appropriate divulgence, nor how I might proceed by any other means at all, and so I say...enough. Merely knowing I've done so much more—and with so little forethought—will be the means to ascertain my triumphs and my failures, whether understood as in or out of some fictive harangue...

φ

I can't recapture what I was when I was there, there on the inside—
when the leaving of the land, that is, contrived a prolix chronicle of
what I would...what I have...I recall now every then as though I knew
what I know now, as though I were as I am now when I was then, with
reference to the cardinal surge of platitudes that stands for all I've
been. There is little more to say of what cannot be said, an assertion
as feckless as it is redundant. What matters is that I go on, that I *have*
done by thinking...by *saying* that I should, and could not turn from
this engagement even were it my wont, a suitor whose compulsion
to seduce is as assuaged by fevered declamation as by tawdry grope.
A snappy reply, the distant murmur of a conscience—what impact,
really, could any of it have on this the feigning syncope of such an
ineluctable decay. I suppose I could have said something, anything
would do, or would have done in coming to this fractured frame,
something to inspire the indifferent benediction of a greater wit than
mine...than that which I can presently recall as having been, but I was
not able then, or I was differently abled, most readily devoted to the
practice of a coward's abdication...

φ

Perhaps I did say something, though how such a surveyor's dictum
could count in the service of that weak-kneed persiflage I cannot say,
or by saying cannot say I've said, a proof of the position. There is
little left to me in this regard; I think I can recall the glottal twist,
the blighter squirm in that apple of a mouth...I think that I said
something...something...though whatever it was it surely was not
subsequently heard. Not that it would matter if it had been; of this,
if nothing else, I have no doubt. The same mantra, it has never been
repeated; I've indulged the repetition only once, only that once, and
any other exile—or soon to be *exiled*—gazing out upon some squalid
Ister might have...would have...*must* have said the same: Nothing is
happening to me nothing is happing to me nothing is happening to
me nothing is happening...

φ

If I could know I said just what I say I said, and now repeat that mumbled cant for one and all alike, then the present recollection would have a different savor, if not a deviation just as present when that present was the measure of its own belated passage, passing presently the same. Having understood the nature of such turgid retrospection I note that what I said is of no consequence; and having seemingly *retracted* what I think I said, I can say now that it would not...*could* not make a difference either way, but for the corollary observation—more than obvious by this point—that I did not say something... *anything* else. And whereas I don't know what I could have done to succor the affections of a retinue incapable of empathy or regard, I have not yet compiled an inventory of all possible utterance, excluding each alternative from my catalogue of possible failures. It is neither my way nor my purpose; I am no more prone to loiter in regret than I am in reminiscence. That I said anything at all I now think rather doubtful, having knowingly—and only just—made assertions to the contrary. I think that what I said I only thought—and thought of saying—for no other purpose than distinguishing the moment for its future recollection—the insipid reminiscence I've attempted to revoke by this untoward inaugural...

φ

I've imagined so much more than I can presently recount, an excess of such magnitude I fear I might never again surface from that supplemental deluge, that deluge of...I imagine so much more that might have been, it's difficult to stop from listing all the inspirations, disparate though they seem, but so I must, and so I will, for dread of having nothing left, and leaving nothing...Everything is excess, always born in excess of the nothing that it ought to be, the null that every happy creed resolves into a dire amnesty. I know I've offered little to justify the pose, but while it's evident I'm willing on occasion to regale with such an incidental sham, I employ the practice only to avoid the cheerless stupor of some avuncular initiate. That I should find a way to think myself that dismal type...it is more than I could do—or *hope* to do—to stay the course...

φ

All I mean is...all I mean...I could not stay, not even if I wanted to, which I did not, no sir, as anyone who's suffered through the passage to majority—who's likewise been expelled from the cruel latency of youth—must understand quite well. That *I* was once ensconced in some apt juvenility I can't be sure, and in any case don't care. I suppose a glum nostalgia for some moment of transition—for *any* of the stages on life's way—could explain much, but such is not the marrow of this wandering reflection, or what I will employ to fill its carcass to the pith; the extravagance might justify some structural resentment—that then I was not as I am, nor as I appear—but this is nothing in support of the necessity of the claim, nor its subsequent defense. It could, that is, explain a change in mien that seems so distant from me now, when all I had considered as my comrades or adherents—as soldiers in the service of the same caustic ideal—had turned that fierce ardency upon their master and their god. At least it might account for why on that one day—and that day first and only—it was time...my *adherents* made it clear it was my time to make my way into the world, a right of passage, as it were, that required neither right *nor* passage...

φ

I was not one of they—of *any* they—from that point forward. Perhaps if I had undergone some similarly prodigious transformation—had been discerned inheritor of some morass of vital schemes—then all of it might make some sense somehow, but I know of no departure that intruded on me then, and once again forego all further speculation on the meaning of such fanciful offenses. Even here, even now, distinctions in the nature and the substance of the subject I inhabit seem purely exoteric when traced back to primal view. There is nothing that has happened—that I have *happened into*—that has not been occasioned by some adventitious plan, an end whose supernumerary trace can go no further in relation—proportional or otherwise—to what I am or will be just the same. Thus I can affirm a voice I would as strenuously ignore had it ever been the fate of any other to endure its remonstrations with me; a voice that proves what it propounds by voicing anything at all—that I am one, and they, yes, they *are all the rest...*

φ

Driven mad, the sea, unable to die in a single wave...It might have all begun this way, I might have made my stand this way, if only I could forget...If only I could remember to forget, I might have finished prior to beginning; I might have started where I now intend to terminate, with what is certain to amount to a considerable increase in efficiency. It will all happen soon enough—the depiction, the confession, the apology, the sanction—a promise sworn upon the virtue of a godhead I know never to have been. Beneath me swells the vesicle of ocean towards the sun, but I am never through it, as it, in it—never finished with the mapping of its mirror *in the One.* To be sure it does not always roar, and at times transcends the incidental reveries of stillness, rising to reconquer empty space; but hours will come when the marchland of the heavens will once again provoke the teeming cosmos to disdain its happy avarice, to swat the lice that crawl across its spewing, limpid sties. Am I not plunging through the interstices of an infinite nothing? Who made this sea a sponge to wipe the sky from its horizon? Butchered worlds, like murdered gods, still spasm in their death throes even after all their murderers have perished...

φ

Some cringing cluck to the bruising skies—and I am back beneath the vault, with neither pale nor shovel to unlock this erstwhile cipher of derangements. So much has passed me by while in the throes of my nostalgia that I feel I must begin again, I must begin anew, I must have since begun anew—and thereby pushed the script that rides this roiling scree to sink beneath some dissipating shallow of a pool. It seems I only ever want for what I need, though never quite as certain at the moment that I need it, regardless if I've chosen in accordance with that ought; I have always done just what I must, though what I do...what I do...There is no one condition that can simplify the gest, nor pull it from the clutches of this manifest uncertainty...

φ

It is of no real importance, whether I must that I will or I will that I must—only that I have...I have begun, for once if not for all, and can at last rest easy in the comforts of the ending all beginnings must assure. Who can say what differential posture any of it marks, let alone that any of it ought; who can tell the doughty desperation of that play against the middle, as though any device has been described as much as promised. And who can tail the drunken tub or armored scow that plods across this tumuli of choking, jellied shallows, to mask the sluggish saunter of some surging volcanism; who can tail that tell but I, I tell of that that only I...that only I can tell alone. If some further standard is required for an ending, for a middle, for beginning where I stand, then let it now continue, that I might find release from my frustrations in the sinkhole of some culpable prospectus...

φ

I say again, I took to sea. There is little less distinguished as a calling or a method, there are few pursuits that beckon any less of their pursuers. Tie a mop to a pig's hoof and strap a concertina round its neck, place a dashing cap betwixt the pink and twitching ears—no more compelling shipmate has graced the deck or galley. It is the tragedy of the seaward life, that any who would take in hand that joust of a harpoon might do as well to slip the point beneath the brow and scrape from greasy fontanelle what little of the gift of reason still remains. This does little, I suppose, to distinguish one who seeks a livelihood at sea from those disposed to estimable industry planted firmly on dry land, as any feckless gentry might inflict the same upon that starboard lobe and find the difference just as difficult to limn—perhaps they all have done exactly that upon the shear effulgence of first light. It would explain much...much more than any other pointed tractate I have come upon by auspice or tuition—to think that I alone was spared such oblique circumcision not by oversight or wisdom, but for the presumed redundancy of the procedure. That any could have ever thought it otherwise...it seems unlikely. I have done little, perhaps nothing, to deter the antipathy with which I am most generally accosted on the lane; and why would it matter, given the incapacity of my peers to distinguish the sapience of an ape from the contortions of its visage...

φ

This nonsense serves no purpose now at all—no purpose here, no purpose now, as though the one could ever be distinguished as precipitate. Why should I be forced to follow an attention that could as prosperously stumble down a most indifferent course? Why should I care, the ape or the sparrow, when each will find its home within a maze of artless toil? I could as easily have lost my way *without* temptation...Such foreboding is a cheap device, but I am no less given to the practice than any other who has taken as their license the crude spelling of a world. Once again I move away from what I was when I first oathed against this mulled prolixity; I am not nothing for nothing, after all. I am not anything for something, I am not not for any ought or naught, nor naught for any yessing yarn inscribed by some flirtation with its terminal sufficiency, the murmuring *poesis* of the main. I am not now, and have not been, the arbiter of any cunning eschaton, nor will I decamp upon some forthcoming parousia to make my dreamy stamp upon the omnibus of history. I am not nothing for nothing, I say again, although the repetition warrants neither preface nor apology—I am not nothing for nothing, nor...

III

Such pleasant office have I long pursued, incumbent o'er the surface of past time with like accord, nor have appeared shapes fairer or less doubtfully discerned than these to which this treatise would direct its fleeting enterprise, a swarm of heady schemes withheld to ease the empty promise of each tutelary barge into the distance. While vowing to provision some beneficent adventure, I have as yet to speak as though there ever were a was to fell that querulous imperil, and in the throes of such malfeasance can't presently decipher the tense of my recounting, so that what's past should be described as passing, while practicing the foresight of what has long since finished. For then as now, I thought it then, how could this brigand's blather measure up against the passage, that allegedly described must of itself be passing in description all the while? If I am now and so I was as I were soon to be, then even the empty pandering of the aesthete would seem to me descriptions to describe describing, nothing more—and *as such* nothing more...

φ

And that is what I thought just then, an inadvertent paean to the runnels of my vocative composures, when clattering up ladders of concocted genealogies I entertained the passage of imaginary comrades into equally phantasmal and suggestive undertakings, each dissolving into the next, an engorgement of narrative contrivances to put to shame the most bathetic almanac of rune or reminiscence. From such suspect consanguinity birthed this simple plan before all other ends received, till the first of all the talking apes did supplicate before me, both hostile and withdrawn, pleading for a chance to launch that doomed and fateful species, the produce of which, I feel reasonably certain, I am just as I was. Imagine the mark of that descent, to think that any life, however innocent and addled, could be worth the hapless prattle of such plenary offense against this cosmic globule of detritus—an insult I'm as sure to carry out by merely breathing. If they could only know; might they beg, might they plead for an ending I alone can aptly render, addressing that ingenuous suppliance to those who serve to mock the fretful form of their descendants, in hopes that they might heretofore be blocked from dipping their limp oars into this insufferable lacuna of declensions by the promise of a consequence their own participation in those prescient transmutations can alone ensure, a whetted stump obliged to split such muling wit from its shuttle of a stour, head rolling off in the shit, blood pooling at the sides of the cave...

φ

And so just then I thought what I was thinking, what now I thought of thinking then, inhumed within a mercy I have not shared with anyone, nor anyone with me, imagining then—as now another apparition speaks—that someday I would put to pad that imagining then, that someday I would put to pad that imagining then, a fabled fold of apes and hunts and shadows, a fabled fold of apes and hunts and shadows. As though for naught I could describe what I have seen and what I've been, but only if the seeing has come first, assuming if I were to spend a simple discipline on anything as rote and understated, I would find the shallow mooring of this mawkish stimulation in its description only, and hastily alight upon what all who are made subject to such tropism assure—that somewhere is that place I will describe, unmediated in its presence, indescribable by nature. So there I stood, thinking that I stood, and that I stood was only stance by a depiction neither willingly nor wittingly preferred, knowing if I should describe it at some next belated landing I would only have described the last description of the posture, such that is as only was and nothing more. And as that future present must adduce *this* speculation, I don't know what could prove I'm not describing the description, always formerly described by the admission that it could be yet described again, and as it could be, thus it must have been...

So great a paradox of structural pretensions I severally arrayed—and did then find I had long since construed—that even now I seem to represent a new assemblage of constituents and fetters, shunt across the brutish divagations of the germ. If I could take up once again that first encumbrance of form, then as a recollection of myself I would not have been stricken with this regress of discrepancies, and could—if only fleetingly—allow that the intransigence from which I here arise should equally surrender its conscripted mendicant upon the altar of the figure I can't help but to abide. If I might somehow differ every *what-I-am* from *that-I-was* then this peculiar discourse would not have since begun at all, and I would remain free, with neither record nor remorse, to stride the brumous mirror of the seas...

φ

All that understood, I am reluctant to regale with feats of gloomy self-deception, and would eagerly return to some thought otherwise contrived—some thought, that is, begun by having ended in its turn. Could I forget the *as-it-were* I was—and chronically as only just—then surely I would start anew, and therewith just the same, described and thus describing the description I've described, describing *in* description what in substance must have always been described at least one time—always at the very least one unremembered time—anterior to this that ever-presently presents it. Should I take it on myself as I am now to willfully forget the *all-I-was* before...before I came to *be* it, then in the now I would still find myself as I was then—but *now*—to strike once again against the simulacrum of the *as-I-was* since then. How could one be anything but lost in such reflection...

φ

Might I straightaway forget what I have since recalled recalling then I would have no reason to recall it in some future passing—passing as if passed—when I should find myself compelled to recollect the recollection now, but in the now that then will be, that culls the fitful pleasures of this unabashed cacophony. It seems so clear—so inescapably *simple*—I wonder how any other stricken with an indecision equal to my own could take up pen as sword and still expect to navigate the taunts and parries of these quandaries unscathed. Such witless youths and simpering savants, whose penning is but reflex to a seizure of the temporal lobe, have preceded me and will as likely trammel in the near, despite all imprecations against intrigues still to come...

φ

What lyric protestations trilled through missive marginalia can adduce the leaky cofferdams of substitute avowals? What drowsy spells and wreathless brows draw nectar in a sieve but think the vessel of creation never full for its immeasurable volume? All this sheathe of windless sail I gather to unveil a lazy paradise of hollows, and for all those who await some stalwart ending to contrive a novel accouchement into that fallen standard, I say I can do nothing to detail the *lusus naturae* at rest within its creature, a redolence sublated by the gilding of the bloom. I wish that I could exercise some sway on those inclined to such indelicate demeanor, commissioning the simplest of fainting cerebrations to prove a sluggish beetle in the brain the only chance of mastering the *techné* of expression. So many have done so much less and called it genius, one would think they'd flock like lemmings to the cliff, a place in that lost history of kindness and gentility assured...

φ

If only I could convince them; the comforting arms of sleep must certainly await; a life in god, for country and for faith, is drawing near, yeah, for all eternity is nigh. A transubstantiation not to lion nor to dove is certain for the same in you that takes you to your end, your glinting and eternal Soul, and wandering the skies from distal verge to apogee, you will be a godlike squall to helixes of twitching froth, vivified to scrutinize thy dreamed peregrinations; neither earth bound, nor as bound to air or water, not of sea nor dirt nor ether will your countenance be made, but cut across the heavens you will fill the cosmic coffer, eternal and decisive, omnipresent and—daring to be brutal in the dauntless course of Nature—without remorse. Go to it, my lovelies, your deliverance awaits—and so shall we be spared another boorish *Bildungsroman*, with verses stretched like sickly leaves to block from all below the nourishment of light and star. Should this discipline seem cruel to some who would account themselves the object of such bellicose harangue—fair enough, I say, what is that to me. For while I may discharge the unapportioned semblance of a means contrived as measure, sizing up the grand collation of that first mephitic capital as mine and mine alone, in doing so I spare each wistful dullard the bleak knowledge of a fate that only I may suffer, for having somehow brought it on myself...

φ

Upon this perch of penance in surrender to reproach I stood to find myself again, and in that stance can yet recall the slithering meridian by which I stood and stand here still—as straining to bound forth upon the topos of my tail, I cannot even fall. I remember it as though I were still harbored in that place, when bolstered by the darkest mood and most impassive aspect—awaiting some inchoate aspiration to befoul the slightest motive that might lead me to pursuit—I thought to let it all go, every striking inference or brief imagining alike, as so much sewage pressing out a glyphic *billet-doux*, a consecration fitted to the pulsating environs; I thought, that is, to bind all turbid wastrels to their youths and manifest such posture as an orphic aggregation of abeyant and repulsive forces, reaching down beneath the feet beneath the cleats composed of skin and twine, where teetering against that newfound balance as if I were released from a confinement I had yet to fully understand, I found myself compelled upright by a third protrusion, neither left leg nor right, but in between and just above the fissure of the fundament...

φ

I can hardly evoke the solace or the promise, neither without reason, but both likewise absented from the clarity of purpose most usually required to secure a stand upon the *terra firma* of mimesis, as sailors buoyed by their sea legs for the first will assume that they were born with the discretion, forgetting that but moments previous they heaved their sick upon the decks like squemish children. The spine, a middling stamen, arched behind so that the weight above that bracing pogo-stick annealment was equal fore and aft, assuring a balance of such unparalleled resiliency that I could have jumped up, kicked my feet out in front of me, and landed in a perfectly stable comportment; I might have been an acrobat of some distinction, had I but been provisioned to achieve such vulgar expertise...

φ

And so as I was lurching...*hopping* on that novel outthrust, I found my own conformity to this most bizarre of phenotypes so peculiar that I began to laugh despite myself, to spite myself, I cannot...I do not know quite which...and so rapturously that even my newfound rudder couldn't keep me upright. I dropped at once to the floor, surging in fits against the legs of the table there before me, and wondering, not all in jest, should I only get a look beneath it for a moment, might it not too possess some prehensile animation, that the pillors kicked from under it would suddenly reveal a parallel appendage, displaying a structural complicity with my own contrapuntal poise that would be nothing short of astounding. Perish the thought, I thought with a wisdom that exceeds my general suasion, but I did not perish it, and just as I realized that my indecision had come to animate the odd proportions of my medial quintessence, I ensured its swift conclusion with a swipe at the two legs closest to me. That the table should have been positioned thusly—that there should have been a table or a floor, or any other scenic paragon to constitute that spectacle of genteel distribution—is not of any consequence whatever; that it was unto itself and still did prove another cipher to endure the hapless hitherto of my inscriptions, so shall it be that every end will follow thought will follow end will follow...

φ

For had I not already been invested with a tail, as one is like possessed of hood or foot or folded talon, of dour mood or shining wing or vapid inspiration? Had I not known the pugilism of my scurvy forebears since I was but a pup, and ridden roughshod in the belly of a shade at once forgotten, with whom I could as surely mate as dine had but the noisome balm of some generic ovulation reached the twitching tenders of my juvenescent snout? Was there not a time upon the prairie or the range when I lounged within the womb but still did suckle at an udder, a puling interregnum on the passage to some transcendental reign? Of this I say that I cannot recall, or that such recollection would return me to its presence—I was not then, I was not there, I cannot take my place within the corsair consecution that my manifest ascendancy requires to account for its untimely consummation, for the odd chance I might come to find some dissolute alterity an equal to my own beleaguered sequence of advancements. I know I shifted to and fro upon a third leg so outrageously proportioned it seemed a languid rigging bound to neither mast nor sail, and in that form I've presently arrived, a hopping punch drunk, incapable of moving one crossed hoof without the other...

φ

The table fell; the table fell atop my thighs; and as the piercing oxidation of a jutting nail found its entrance there, so did my phlegmatic laughter turn a truculent color indeed, with a sneer and a crook and a bawl and a weep. It may well take a long tradition of vice to associate pleasure with the consciousness of pleasure, but pain and the consciousness of pain are identified even in the idiot. Thus every twinge effected by that ferrous, bitter thorn—pictured now as still, as without movement or stillness—could only be precisely represented through a winnowing of nerves equivocally offended, at least if those inclined to monitor these glib proceedings hope to try the same upon themselves and have the same I've had. It seems unlikely, nonetheless, that any allied malformation of the spirit or the flesh will come upon the table and the nail, as well the floor beneath, and should the caudal branch I've only just recalled discovering, recalled recalling all the while...should that furling haunch have itself taken the blow, how would a taxonomy of the electric impulse coursing down its length help to describe the sense to one who's been denied the stately pleasures of that atavistic adjunct, that protracting breach...

φ

This was not so, it was not so, but for my purpose here, it might have been. For can the leg be said to move by similar momentum when that limb belongs to one denied such tertiary gift? Were it but the mangled outcrop of some freakish efflorescence could the form of any other blubber sheathe the sense I sense again in each recounting of it—of one's *possession* of it in proportion to its reach? All in all it all seems far less likely for the repetition; thus I turn back from the reminiscence, back again to lie within the wallow of the present, to roll and flinch upon the scrum of that inflated currency, where I might once and finally conclude my indecision and advance…

φ

I want to say…I *only* want to say I tell just what I am, I am just what I tell, so the tail extends behind me, and forthwith I stand. I want that the nail piercing the thigh should be felt as I felt it, which as point of reference functions as a model of the telling, and whether or not it ever has been known as such to any other has had no influence upon, neither against, the content of what's told. Or perchance, again, by that selfsame assertion…statement… *conclusion*—whatever the conatus of this distended mode—it all remains incapable of taming the course of my conclusory digressions, for having since revealed the tell I am—or will be soon—precisely as it is, and not by an appeal to what or *that* it so prefers…

φ

An obtuse retrospection to be sure, and just as necessary as not; I am that I tell I am, even should my raillery profess to have described another…another *it* as I may ever be. I don't know if this wayward repartee displays the eager plaint of some first freedom or restraint, and that is not my problem or affair; I'm not concerned that it ensures my servitude to doggerel—that I find myself again interred within some torpid cynosure of scumbled cant and descant—as either way, in either case, there is no difference to it. One may surmount the distant peak by ratchet hook and cordage, or merely drop from greater heights upon the serried ridge, but whatever means employed to take one's place upon the apex, the vertigo is equally unnerving, or sublime...

φ

For myself I declare that as I stood I fell, and as I fell the table fell atop me, as so did an extrusion of metal, left unattended for who knows how many centuries, enter into my thigh with considerable discomfort. All strange away did there appear a close coagulant surround, hardening with such speed and delicacy I then and there assured myself that this would be the sixth appendage, an appendage's appendage, as a carbuncle on the cheek or a branch hung off the bough. I am, it seems, quite prone to such assumptions, as even the most impotent adhesive—the glue of reasoned recollection—mires me so desperately within an unfelt otherness that soon enough I come to think it as a portion of myself, extending out upon the dilating horizon until I am as all and all is one. How then to describe the description, or the intellect that immures it just the same? How attain the promised ease of some dogmatic slumber with the isomorphic bracken of the sea stuck to my hull, as the colonization of some otherworldly fungus? Thus the hairs that grow from follicles still cleaving to the skin—and futhermore the vestments set to unconceal an inch or two of villous, scaly limb—appear to me but each another stuttering insentience born viscid into sward, or into...

φ

So many times I've thought of simply shaving myself bare, to seem but one more scrap amidst the refuse of some tawdry cosmic whimper. What reason not to purge oneself of all that's dead and thus display one's élan vital undeterred? And as the words, the proclamations, the scriptural barbarisms sputter off the throated wheel like vitreous sugar twisting into lace, do they appear not just as dead, the decorous remainder of a life that never was, or never should have been? No, it is not this sort of anima that proves the censure of the vital, nor some fleet invagination to accomodate the influx of some proteinaceous cipher, but an animation of the senses, touched and touching, the vigilance of even the most languid rumination spun about the spindle of its transubstantial skein...

$$\varphi$$

Every eminent aseity becomes again the alter that has always been the substance of its brutish sensitivity, decaying into something just as other as again, thus distinguished from its no less constant given. I decay within myself; but my expressions—though they may appear precisely what and as I've come to seem—once they are expressed are nothing but another cast off pupa, berthed upon the raiment of an evanescent din. That moment that I am, of stratagems and quaking molecules, extends only to the limits of sense, and as it trails off further it moves closer to the periodic cipher of the otherwise that constitutes the traction of inherence, the tractable resistance of the *in*. One need only tug upon a goiter for it to be my own, and pull me by the shirt and there the fabric seems a second skin; likewise strike my hands with a deadening of nerves and they will cease their pained alliance with the rest...

$$\varphi$$

I say it now, perhaps again; this tail of which I've spoken only briefly first disclosed its flailing advent at the moment I recall beginning,... begin recalling...it appeared at that one moment as if presently arisen from the furrow stricken fundament I am as much encumbered by, and did so to my great surprise, as if I were recalling then its absence from all recollections previous. But this is misleading; for while I may recount my consternation as some other expectation was betrayed, I still can't look back further than those transitory spasms of a consciousness preceding that bewilderment—there is nothing to me now but those brief moments just before—and as the time past since exceeds its quantity by so great a measure, it is as though the blinking of an eye and nothing more...

φ

It might be known as easily by such inchoate testimony as by the schizoid monadology of descriptive reportage; while neither will suffice as sacrament or severance, both at once can limn a speculative portraiture more ably than any pedantry devoted to the most high... In the cradle of this impotence I've managed to continue on—continue now—as ever I have, and done so by the same remorseless hesitancy that started me upon this vapid précis, lived but still untold. For as I lay upon the floor, imagining a grainy wood where linoleum should perish, and as it seemed the new and jagged follicle of rust had come to rest in proper order just the same as any other obtuse entrance into thigh, so did another leg of the beastly parastasis give way at the joint of a withered, creaking juncture, plunging as a leaden lure to plumb the darkling depths of a cavernous trough...

φ

The second leg gave way upon the same hinge as the first, without the slightest shear or sway of turbulence above it, and with it did the sharpest pain wrench point up on another slant, to split the length of hide upon the striping of the implant and force a new striation of the thigh. If flesh were only flesh and blood only blood, then neither would have ever held their own against the other, and the transduction of atmospheres would have driven the bearing of ten thousand insides out upon the dusky shallows. But these that are are not themselves distinct from these they're not; it's as close as I have come to the transcendence of the ego since adducing the infernally porous crapulence of this waxing gloss. That these are not these but one, and on the one go strapping over sodden moor and graven glance, to find in every trespass a desecration of one and all alike, the same nail the same prick the same blood the same flesh...

φ

Like so each one appeared to me not as one at all, but as the same plurality that all such oneness forwards as a rigid plain, a binding caul; one nail into one flesh, and forthwith I felt equal to all other subitaneous defilements. And while the discovery of an odd proportion here or there may for an instant—and did at the arrival of that prehensile protuberance—distract from the wholeness of any future anamnesis, it compares by analogy only to the irruption of that which remains wholly extrinsic, through which I feel nothing and exact no willful discharge. How can one consider the gross paralysis of forms when all seems to itself a whole, as some cranial malaise contrived to keep the boorish Platonist from reading the true World Soul through the entropy? I will not suffer the indignities of such an obsequious fallacy, apologizing to the grand spirit of Gaia with every brooding cudgel of a leap...

φ

Then as well as every now since then I knew forsooth; I extend only as far as the projection of the senses, and no further will I ever range, even as the fragile prancing of causation takes me out upon the infinite like a God—with every twitch I pine against the orbital influence of galaxies, pulling this or that most precious speck from the visage of some pulsing star. It is mine only if it is mine alone; even were the repetition of such dulling sentiment able to contribute to the gramary of an inscrutably uncommon understanding, how, I ask, would this sacrosanct dissemination of univocal afflatus distinguish mine alt service to the Grecian abstract from that of the most simple-minded proselyte? For this and this alone allowed me to tear the nail from the thigh and the thigh from the nail, sobbing and cursing and pleading with each labored breath beneath that straining carapace of conscience...

φ

So I pushed into the table, thrusting palms and thorax into splintering veneer, of alder or of basswood, a granular integument set to couch a peeling picture of the cheapest pine, as a queue of cigarette burns pressed into the swimming density of particle board. And there the first three fingers of the left hand, counting the middle as the third, blanched to pull so many riven splinters...well, not that, but rather did the bits of tattered cellulose enter the prints of the first three fingers of the left hand, along and between the tethering striations that make them so, that make them prints, that is to say; the other hand I held in place behind me, forgetting for an instant that I might as well push up with tail as arm, and have as a support the other hand, the right hand in its turn. The recollection of the fifth limb nonetheless inspired a response as lamentable as contrary, that I should—and did as should—push the right hand palm into the table, flat upon its bottom, just as I had the left hand hitherto, but for the pulling back of all attendant digits of that hand, such that the first four fingers of the right hand—counting the pinkie as the fourth or first—thrust out as an anchor through the pitching surf of air, as did the first finger—first by name alone—of the left…

φ

This gullible repulsion served its purpose well enough, a proof against the premise that provoked it—that the print of the finger had some-how drawn the fragmentary peel into its ridges, even as the metal below began to yield to the grudging lubrication of the wound. Still did one thick blade of cellulose press rigid into palm, perhaps upon a crease, perhaps between and into the most shallow of impressions. Perhaps, I thought, perhaps. Perhaps if such a mottled violation of the flesh had crossed the plane of palm along the line, then indeed the crumbling minutiae interred within the digits of the left hand could have entered in relative proportion to the distance between striations of a certain depth, the figure formed to that effrontery thenceforth measured and predicted by the distance between each marked indentation and the next—any other deemed as next—on the palm, that is, on the palm…

φ

I had not long been seized by this odd series of befuddlements when an image of the daemon—of some erratic seraphim—appeared before me and flickered away, leaving in its absence a defiantly im-mutable resolve. I recall it only in the interest of science, an interest presently of little interest at all. And so I'll say no more of this pecu-liar form of exigence, but that I was therein made mindful of a critical coincidence of offenses; that as one mass exited the flesh, so did countless others enter, each discrete by density and weight, traveling a peculiar course that seemed to follow from inorganic to organic, as though some itemized Galapagos of recollections. Thus to excoriate the fittingly self-conscious convolutions of another infarcted understanding, allowing all my faculties to slide into receivership; not a one is better fit to cipher such a science of the ordinary than another, as each is as incapable of conjuring the register of filial divergencies required to describe that inconsolable perdition...

φ

If one *must* apply this sort of execrating praise in order to repudiate the means to its expressed regard—an expression that might otherwise go on and on and on without the simple stopper of the simplest rebuke—so be it; it matters all the same—which is to say, *not at all*—to any other rarefied uniquity whose substance is constructed like my own. It seemed to me that if I had continued to engage this flailing regress of defenses the advancment of intrusions would multiply in turn, and only by the increase would each assimilation of the flesh seem more as a coincidence of spasms than an excitement of the nerve. I could only imagine the expansion—beyond reason, *against* reason—that as such deft mimesis is enacted *by* reason its potency cedes back to the inertia of refractory resolve, by which that consummate lucidity would cease to consume anything at all, but be consumed, as all, by all, against all, all the same. What a vain and torpid ruler is this fellowship of faculties, this evanescent practicum one fashions as a *selfdom*, that to locate its nature it must conceal the same, and only in that dormancy lay claim to some last first identity again, an eminence pressed into this insoluble imperium from what else but the other side, the other side...

φ

This first of many lessons in the inertial physics of my own ill-composure had within it some not inconsiderable animus, and by such artful practice I knew I might portend to meet that presence full and without equal; I knew, that is, that should the nail return to that inertia from which this alliance had arisen, and should the table take as an inventive purpose all its own the disencumbrance of the flesh that others seek by way of prophecy or sacrifice, then so my own discomfiture would dissipate in turn. And does it now seem clear, should it not have all along…could I have only seen what I saw then through the refraction of some later then, as that past now is just as then as any then before…Shouldn't I have always grasped that no one privileged trespass can be reconciled to or through the tenuous alightments yet revealed by every deference to the form of the intrusion thus distinguished? Have known that what accounts for the internment of the counter in the counting is itself always unseen but for the bourne of that dispersal in and as whatever must have been, what must remain…

φ

Here—at least *herein*—is nothing not unsaid; surely I must tire of the suave discontinuities I've otherwise contrived to frame this cunning lapse *sans gêne*, and can as well dismiss all similar concerns from further mention, but for the fateful missive here recanted as recalled. If only the perspicuous descent of this dismissal could justify the sophistry from which it since has issued, then indeed I would say nothing more of it, as now there would be nothing more of it to say. But this apparent expostulation—this *expositive appearance*—does nothing of the kind; nothing but suggest an absence still to be *filled in* by the discretion. Such clever jargon reconciles longing to accomplishment, and it is by this understanding that I speak so brightly and without confusion. Thus I realized that the garden path was weeded in a circle, and in the walking of its outline I might somehow come to know another *in*. It's what I did, it's what I'd do, and doing it as did I will…

φ

Push up against the table, push the thigh into the table, push the nail into the thigh, push splinter into palm and into finger, by neither force of leg nor palm, unmoved by hand or arm or foot or finger, but only pressing into it by pressing down that adjunct furthest from it—

that never once could touch the table, and did not as it couldn't—
did I push out from beneath the table, by pushing up into the table.
For there I pushed into the table, pushed my trunk into the table,
and with the arching leverage of that preternatural spindle pushed
off against the table as I pushed into the table, and in one continu-
ous movement the table arose thither into sky, and towards the sky I
looked, my tail turned down to push up without nearing any plateau
of the kind, and without pressing towards the table, but still against
the runnels of the undulating floor, as there I rose upright again, sup-
ported not by hand or leg or table, leaning in to test the novel balance
of a new age, and the table fell in front of me as all things fall away...
all fall away from torso and hand and thigh pulling nail and splinter
and flesh, and pulling nail and splinter from the greater part of the
flesh while taking with it some tithe no less painful for its portion, it
all came down a clattering heap upon the lifeless plain before me...

φ

And so I balanced there before the clatter as it clattered, resuming a
pose of such striking and forthright pugilism that neither mammal
nor marsupial could sidle near enough to instigate the pleasures of a
sterile copulation—a speculative claim, but no less likely to be true
for the refusal to provide conditions for its verifiability. Perhaps, I
thought, this agile bulge of coccyx will ensure my fate is on the
butcher's board, just that once and for the last to seize upon another
view, to take some ersatz luminescence spread across the welkin to be
the pentimento of some long forgotten master stroke. And what if I'd
begun with that pieta of an *idée fixe* alone? It's where I am, if nothing
more, and that must be enough to presently move on—enough of
what, I still can't say, but sure enough enough of something there can
be enough of...

φ

It may be I'm the only one afflicted with the yearning that results in
such repulsions and attachments, but what of it; why would any other
grant a more precocious privilege; why not kneel before this whited
sepulcher to light its unseen shrine for an ostensible eternity; who

better to apply an exsiccating salve to the viscid flesh of the word in-nominate, alight within a belly set to dive the depthless fathoms of this rambling enclosure; who could be more suited to such languor in the cradle of a void without a frame, so to sally onward with a simple-ton's remorse—and thereby share one's last adventures to the last, the very last. So many clues may serve to undefine this latent birthright; I might well take to some dissembled anarchy of eddies as to any hal-lowed mount supplied with expiating altar and still think myself the hero of adventures worth recounting as a life, but this cataract of rev-enant mementos has carried me to quite another end...

φ

And still no wiser for it, with nothing hence acceded to a greater wit than mine, the tortuous credo of a mumbling idiot is all that any pleasured speech has since appeared to me, and I am as I've always been—decidedly, abidingly alone. Had I not found my place within that solitary fellowship both at and for the sake of that same solitary mode—I have, I did, I will it to be so—or failed to understand the ease of my impassive balance when the table fell atop that squirming surfeit of the sacrum, to throw it off again by some insoluble passiv-ity, then I think that I would lie there still, to trill the same electric every maggot whistles on the way from worm to fly, a chased field cut across the curdled spume; I might have never come to be, I might have never been, if not for all I've since appeared to every henchman or adherent struck dumb by the distant turn from exile to intern-ment, all I ever was before the advent of this moment, alone alast the lone last goggle of the lidless eye, skewered to the flaccid sail...

IV

I couldn't then have known what course my life would take—if I can rightly call it that, a life, that is, or a course, as though I could have hearkened to the one without the other. By then, at then, the now that I was then, when first I heaved that coverlet of cellulose from off the pained communion of conjunctions I had only just discerned— had just discerned discerning, if not a more accomplished claim. So many cruel and crudely fraught adventures have I led, that any one should stand out as preamble to the rest...I don't know how to justify this choice of consecution in particular, but for the realization that avowals of exception serve as the effect—and not the cause—of such proximal quiddity. I have never vouched an understanding I don't presently possess, or a reflection I have not performed by stride or supplication; it may seem so much nonsense, this visionary prattle, but still I find my peace in the limpidity of sense alone. It's all I've been, it's all I'll be, admitting that I've never once conceived the slightest choice...

φ

Thus *accepting* this acceptance of my sanguine acceptation, I'm certain I've been something...somehow something more than only that. I am the tell of what I never was and never will, always moving on before I've seized a bounding terminus in the word or the flesh or the name or the name of the word or the flesh or...What of it is there left. By saying it I've garnered nothing but the saying of it still, describing what evades description by having yet to indicate its mire of fixations. What I mean—what I think to mean to tell—is that everything I've been is so much less than what I'll be, and that is little enough to think it worth the toil of any next consideration, however one might be refreshed by such a static spray...

φ

Well enough...I say it well enough, and carry on like some distended prophet of the firmament with every labored wheeze, the blighted ocean of an oculus closing in around the pod and crux I stab into the scree. I know I did arise just then, and have found myself not there again, never once in that first place again, upon the shallow pier my window looked upon, as much a desert as a plain for all the caps of fluid hillocks folding into foam, every plummeting meringue set up to circumscribe the mantle of its dissipating film, to think myself most adequately fixed and fitted out for this—or *that*, that is—cuirass of feckless purposes alone. Not to gaze, but to take—to take the sea by taking to a vision of its fringe, and have it as my own to thereby bind myself within...

φ

I can nearly now recall how it all transpired, set against the labors of quotidian contortions. Bending at the waist and stiffening my tail, I hoped to push the torso upright, ignoring that in such a state I could not balance on the left leg, the wounded leg; *forgetting*, that is, the peculiar discomfiture attendant to all wounds left unencumbered by the scab. What a benediction this protuberance did prove! It is difficult enough to recollect such efforts without contempt, let alone transcribe the profits of mimesis while shielding from the brackish splash the vellum covered with the scrawl, and so all tamed expression disembogues into the bleary drought from which it must ascend, a prison of ink alone composed by those who think to lock its gates, meaning everything that means at all, but suggesting nothing other than itself. If I could only take it back, take any of it back, as though there's anything to stop me...

φ

If I could have the same again, again I would not travel from this disaffected homily to such perverse conclusions. It can hold no real significance to any other but the other I remain, indistinct from any other other likewise gone astray. I'm not sure how to start describing such a transitive alterity, when that description must unmask the always ever outside...I have not tried, or I have not tried *successfully*, which I like to think a tautological assertion, and though I may have gazed across the quivered crepuscule of this abysmal sham, and done so not the once or twice or thrice to stake the deictic scribble of a dictate I have only just begun, I can't portray a singular encounter with that trembling abyss as anything but that—as an absence, or an equivalence of absences. It is a complication...a *difficulty*, if you will, I have not reckoned with the rule of sense or reason; it may be I'd regret it either way, but I won't seize the prospect here, not now, for fear that I might have to end it all and that it all might end by some lewd discharge of adroit solicitations. I'm not that sort of popinjay, a dandy of a philosophe so taken with my querulous composures—as well my compositions—that it's possible to think I could end anything at all, let alone begin it. Let it alone, I say, and nothing will require nothing of nothing, and I may finally be on my first and final way...

φ

And while I prance along this gulch as though I were within it—as though I'd ever known it as it was, as it is, as it will be—I cannot speak of any path endured without contrition and resistance, or tell of any taken with a prideful thumping of the thorax or a slap across the knee. If I were to start again I'm not certain that I'd do so any differently, that I'd know the form of tail or pate as any sort of deference towards a less fortuitous ancestry, or that I would have settled in the shipyard, say, or any other commonplace locale, and never thought or claimed to think to go to sea at all. It means little to disclose it, I know that I've said nothing of the venture or such doughty leanings, other than recalling the first discovery of the tail—the tell of the tail and only that, and that alone. Nonetheless I verge upon some more distinguished farce, to face the gamboling temptation that remains—as ever it has *seized*—the errant stillness of the pulmonary push and suck, suck and pull, holding steady on the precipice, knowing that the leap can only promise a diversion as exciting as it is brief; and swaying to and fro upon that ragged precipice I cannot even fall, for the clench of my own tail upon the brink...

φ

Why I should bother to gather any portion of this chaste and mealy inventory I cannot say, or rather, while I can, I will not, I will not say it here, not tell it now, it does not suit my purpose in the least... *as* the least or in it, either way. Even this revelation seems to me a surrendering of too much—too great a clue against the puzzle of a survey hardly started—but I will not take it back, for having done as much already and thought the subsequent disparity negliglible, scarcely worth the trouble of this tedious reproof. That I might have a purpose of the kind, of any kind at all, really—let the furtive dabblers who profess to know the difference sort it out; perhaps I have always begun, perhaps I will always begin...in the middle, already in the middle, a spark that finds its purchase in returning to the flame from which it sprang...

φ

I recall a limping, a rising...I recall some recollection of the kind, though the difference between the two—between the recollection and the recollection of the recollection—eludes me now just as it ever did; if I could somehow gather my wits back into this shelter of ripostes, then so I would have done, and here I would be done with it for good. But I know nothing of what I know nothing of, and while the presentation of my erudition might seem as clumsy as it is transparent, it holds little relevance to an understanding of what it is I am or do, despite my efforts to codify this duly hindmost futurition once its done. By what it is I am I am, by that I am I am, and for the promise of this always next collection of collections I cast myself distractedly away, like some ecstatic pig on the scent of the next truffle, forgetting that the last was seized as soon as it was found; *hoping*, that is, to forge some novel method to consume what I have gathered, a scheme I know I can't enact for the constraints of the muzzling...of the muzzling...of my ever more distinctly porcine muzzle...

φ

All such execrable lineaments aside, I think I can awaken something more than that lame discharge from a tyranny of planks, a limping, a rising, a lying down or something of the kind, it looms as through a magnifying loupe held backwards to the eye, a graven aberration that seems to gather all space in a single point. I recall a gaping outlet to that radial arcanum—an egress from the distance to the nearness of the scene—though why it was arranged as such, what forelimb cut an aperture from that stucco imbrication I can't say, for having not a single recollection of its span. I remember the window, or I remember the view, without a pane or panel there to cut across its isthmus, nor pitted floor to saddle ever over or subjacent or against, and yet...

φ

I was there. I was there at the window, I was there at the opening of the world, to spy a boundless sea and shattered pier athwart its heaving precincts as upon, a fallen, shabby berth presiding over every ruinous clap of surge and gale, as some angelic minion wary to ascend for fear their dim adherents would be lost to some long prophesied indenture in their absence. And bobbing in that feeble mount was my quiescent tub, amassed with glaucous swells as darkly cast as any plume—the night, as they say, wherein all crows are black—flocked without a flap atop and through and pushing into each the same that stood above it and against; the same, that is, that I should ever think to find my long lost ticket punched. It was there for me, it is there for me, and I will take it where it will, and where it will go so will I, convinced that I would find that fabled polity of wise restraints by taking on the hazards of the main...

φ

A rubbled barge, comprised of clay, perhaps of coal, and either way its hold filled to the limits of its frame, the fetid stores of some lost liege held steady on the hump of that supposed buoyancy—if not, that is, distinctly set upon the silt of sodden shallows, appearing that much deeper for the obfuscation of all sight lines to the bottom. It was my guiding vessel, my determining proposal; I would take that fulsome ship to sea and jump upon its boards to set it free upon the dunes of undiscovered channels. And if it were to sink, I thought, well what is that to me. I fear no ending in the drink, I've always been directed towards such resolute imperil, and decided then to resist it not a moment longer. If I had hitherto done anything, if I had ever done anything, then I realized I would carry on to something else entirely, the last of all conquistadors equipped to beat the shiftless yore of carrion divinity to shore, to meet the de-accession of the signatory dream that lies behind the shuttered porthole of the sundered void...

♀

The problem—the *only* problem—is that I've never been composed of any other nature, and having failed to service such divergent fortune or disgrace, have only done what I've done since—the tell of a tub, but this time blessed with such a stickling and prehensile plug, I cannot find the means to sink beneath the fluid corpus of the waves. That barge was but another lilting Lorelei of failures wrecked upon the twists of rebar locks; if I'd done anything else—had recollected this or that assemblage of such doings having *been* done—then I could work towards something other as again, some otherwise compelled beyond my store of feckless ken, but it was not so, it was not my fate. And though I do not wish to consecrate the reference by attributing some measured or specific gravity—measurable or specified—to its works, the imperative is always only a relation to the *in-itself* defiled by its efficacy, and in this respect is indistinct from any other transcendental ought. What I mean...what I mean is...is only that there must be something there...there must be something for there to be a there at all, and I have not found it, I have not held that ball of wax between my clammy palms, nor permitted it to deliquesce upon some newly sprouted tongue. It does not matter what the mark or vestige of some imitative novelty; it's just that...it's only that...I have imagined so much—*doing* so much—that now I can't distinguish what I have from what I haven't, what I could but somehow didn't, what I was from what I weren't...

φ

Nothing's going to happen, I'm sure of it now; nothing is happening to me. Nothing's going to happen that hasn't happened already, all that's happening has happened, and anyone who'll ever come to pass through this same hatch of supplications has already finished—by having thrown themselves upon the mercy of this vatic scam; what I am saying now is not being said by me, but is dug up from the ground like a grain of petrified wheat, to seed the same remorse and till the same accomplishment to seed, as if there never was a were...were a was that ever was or were a was or were at all. At all or to all, I do not care what preposition such a proposition has its naming sounded through, or out, to prove the point, I do not care because it does not matter—at least not to my present rise or coming fall...

φ

What does, I presume, presented twice or thrice already, as though I were to stake my claim to such urgent distinction by following the spoor of so many comparably frenzied recollections, so many supervenient sodalities and mirthless reminiscences, a maunder ever bounded by this fugitive preamble to its profligate economy of discharge... There is little to any of it that has not been said before, there is none of it, forsooth, that I have not said before...One might consider this dissemblance the babble of a fool for its redundancy alone, and while I have indulged no prolixity to speak of, to speak of anything at all can purpose to produce no more than such prosaic glossolalia, made palatable only by accession to this pageant of alliterative wiles. All by way of introduction, I have given nothing to get nothing, and by that churlish gift has each alterity within arisen to disclose the yawning passage at my back...

φ

What matter is a prayer pitched to a furrow in the breeze, an image of the demiurge cast as a cataract of fragments? What significance a sacrifice to one whose nature is engendered by the portent of the sacrifice itself, as though an endless interruption could be equal to an ideal continuity? What end...what end will such beginnings proffer as pro-cure for a maker born of plank and nail, with a thigh for an anvil and a precipice the model for the workings of the world? What subject does this scripted welter carry in its womb, a confinement undesired but accepted for the promise of a trickling miscarriage? What dif-ference...what difference at all to an inquiry without the expectation of response, what equivocation draws this *what-I-am* from out the seething luxus of its ontic extract, the condensation of some elemen-tal aspect from the certitude of every dullard's froward superfluity? What differs the terror of meaning from the whimsy of its semblance, the mark from its impression on the palimpsest beneath...

ϙ

It may seem foolish to begin this way, as well to end, I cannot...I *do* not take exception to the grievance—but what other choice have I? None, I say, for having thought it first, then twice and thrice, and thought to call it foremost, even as a secondary claim. So much has come before—and that...all that I've smuggled past my jailers with the rest of the rubbish. A wistful trope that yet contrives another ci-pher; I am not watched, I have never been subjected to such vigilant surveillance, there is no rubbish, I do not make that sort of difference *happen*, as the affect of judgment or the defect of consumption, I do not make it so I cannot shroud myself or my emoluments within it as a method of escape. Or rather, there is nothing *but* such rubbish, but the same folderol of faculties and hoaxes I've employed to fuel the recollection of a first that never was—that never could have been... But I get ahead of myself, and it's a race I'm not comfortable winning. I thought just then just what I thought just then, I think I thought it then though now is hardly some great distance from the advent of that seemingly imperishable toil; it's clear that now that now is noth-ing but another then, still a then though then it was as much a now as now is, as any now is...

ϙ

I thought to take to sea just then, the nail was out all right, and I had found the greatest purpose ever that I would above the surging mizzenmast, a monkey in the crow's nest, my most adept appendage clinging to the spar where any other lost in that same reverie would find their fate fulfilled upon the pounding surf below; hovering above Descartian vortices, I hold my carcass steady by the ordinal exuberance of my tail—strung up by my own tail—without a heed to future fate or fortune. Never has appeared a more agreeable acquisition! If I could only know the means by which I'd been invested with that salutary bane, certainly I would share it...I would have already... and subsequently left this torpid chronicle right where it began, with nothing and as nothing, to swallow up the names of all things named, stuck in the craw as some obscenely swollen membrane, melting with such sluggish delectation one would never again suffer for a gustatory need...

φ

If I could tell of something else then that's what I would do...what I would have and would still...admitting that my confidence in this assertion is quite feeble, for never having had the chance...I suppose I might contrive myself the subject of this lame detachment and escape—lame and limping, a gimp for all reasons—but it is not so, it is not my way. It is all I know or have known; one might proffer either postulate without discernible effect. That I might have known...I might have...and forgotten—it seems I can't delineate the difference between such pitiable state and having never known at all. All these beggar's choices appear equally ill-suited to the cause that I appear to no less champion, a pose of penance and remorse; it seems impossible to imagine I could forget so much had I ever really known it, or that I could have ever not known more than it appears I know right now...

φ

One can't recork that bottle once the stopper's out, and although I'm not the one who opened it—an assertion only properly understood with the caveat that I wouldn't admit it if I had—the silent effluvium of sick and fermentation is splattered on the canvas like an oil slick, with every inky beast and beastly apparition rising from its muddled mire of a wake, the pathetic slapstick of a breathless flounder flailing in that unctuous brew. I recollect the room, I don't know why or wherefore, or by what means I was engendered through or into such a pestilential hole, a deft transfiguration cast of terminal disquiet, thrown into the vertigo of stasis, then collapse. There is nothing else here now...*other than* here now that might confer the status...the mark of any here or there at all, and though I languish *there* no longer, I am at least still here, stretched along the nimble supinations of my tail. There have been others here and there...here or there...such voices ring through this assent as stones thrown down a wishing well, a splash of silt and sewage drying thick upon each froward glance into its heedless scowl...

φ

As if to put a visage to that chiseled, fearful mien, the quaver of a throat to guard against a coming song; this echo with no maiden call, this repetition without first—it's how I've come upon this turgid rictus. And my altar, presently displayed as some obscene exuberance curled up at my fundament, is my tail alone, meaning I'm the only one precluded penance or purgation at its use. Only I, that is to say, have never bent before the lithe propeller at my back, the caudal idol of a new age, writ large by the portent of this monarch without court, this blowhole that has never driven carcass into tidal wash— what difference could it make to one who isn't burdened with such savage gifts as these. What difference could it make...could make the world the sense I am—or have, that is—what difference could make or could have made the world the sense I have or am—I have *as* am— what difference the mute stipulations of this unattributable sham, never formerly conceived as such a terminal dispensation. I will not go that way, I will not tread the path laid out by some disdainful orison or deferntial vow, for nothing other than the obdurate resilience of collateral adherents tied into the decussated nerve. If there were ever any other worshiper to speak of, then perhaps...but it is not so, it has never been, as far as I know, or can recall, which amounts to the same thing, the same difference, each the same...

φ

Convened against the gilded maw that heaves this furtive gleam I say—what is last is first and first is last, and so hope to fulfill the lineal requirements of this eternally protracting *auto-da-fé*. If I could only recollect how it was framed, or how I fit within it, I might provide the recipe without further haste or forethought. But I have only that floor and that window and that barge, only that unyielding tableau left to yoke the force of wind and sail upon my cloying journey through the midden of the world; I have only the drift of limestone and of limed earth to mark my progress, and that...all that—taken in the aggregate—is little enough to designate such difference as effect...

φ

The more I understand the worth of this insuperable adjunct, the more I deplore my failure to represent its mastery; nonetheless I gird myself against such facile disaccord, and continue on my indirect assemblage of the passage, to search for a lost word, to lift sick eyelids, and with lime-corroded blood gather grasses for an alien tribe. Soon enough they will begin to gather, a congregation of the sort of swindlers most inclined to advocate some legerdemain as the charter of a god, to see not in that appanage the putrefying figurement that is their warp and wont alike. The status of such depredation is only granted those who are like fewer than they are unlike, and so is the role reversal I have hitherto resisted made complete. I have always been compelled to aberration of the kind, expressed by what appears some cardinal pretense to the contrary, and despite having proved myself superior by both somatic wit and mental acrobatics— as though the one could ever be distinguished from the other—I take my place within that lost menagerie of clayscapes and retorts without complaint, for the pacifying easement of expectant supplications that only the next exile is granted for the effort, or the easy gest...

φ

And who better for it, who else so well suited to the casting off...the casting *out* I'd joyfully initiate had it not been imposed upon first light. If I could have it any other way, that is, I simply *wouldn't*, supposing this confession could be taken at face value, given in the context of so much other sham contrition and compliance. I bristle at the thought of such obliged verisimilitude, the lacuna that manifests my hesitant attempts to calibrate the force of what will never be against the stasis of what never was; I am only as I will be—it has always been sufficient to embody the inertia of my leaden pace. I suspect there is no state that would not meet this barren standard, and the failure of any effort to falsify the claim—or provide a rubric that would qualify its referent as more than definitional—is not lost upon me...

φ

It is nothing to me to be as I am, it means nothing to know that I'm enough of what I am, for the incapacity I display with every wandering despondency against that ineluctable sufficiency—which is to say I can't conceive my dissonance by any other mechanism or in reference to some newly formed or foundering ideal. Not to suggest I'm satisfied...*repleted* with such potage; how could I not *not* be, if any other ever is...any who has found their approbation in the postulate ontogeny I've always been denied. And though I am aware that no similar disposition can body forth an answer to this intrinsic ask, I do not care, I cannot, I will not, I never have; I want for nothing more, or rather, I ask for nothing more than what is evidenced by this fond interrogative, the grasping thievery I achieve with every silent finger slipped into the stranger's sacral pouch or pulsing purse of promontory brow, the pickpocket of metaphysicians and nihilists alike...

φ

I wish I could be more forthcoming; it can come as little comfort... it is little comfort *to me*—an evasive response to a rhetorical posed as a conditional. Whatever it is I hide, that is, I hide it even from myself. How do I know, then, that I have hidden anything? I don't—not by the standards of discernment most usually employed to judge the probity of such heroic premises. This fallacy emboldens into praxis my elusive lucubrations; I have hidden something, I say again, from myself as much as any other, the one feature I'm certain I share with that species of wound from which I somehow issued, if my slouch alone can intimate my having once belonged to such a kind. I am compelled, that is to say, in fulfullment of an appetite I won't describe as anything but a lack...*by* anything but this absence of description...yes, I say, I must mean something...*have meant* something, I'm sure of it, there is no other promise to account for my appearance in or as this manner of declension...

φ

I am too little and I am too late; I have never signed for revelations sent to me by post, nor practiced to completion the sacerdotal onanism of a collar cinched too tight—too tight, at least, to coax even the shallowest of breaths from the dilluted haze that circumscribes the lookout's lofty perch. I am nothing if I am not this, this counting and recounting, this presence and this absence, this tail that slaps the back and whips the groin to parry visionary thrusts, that keeps the wasps from nesting in the bowl of any cecum slit to gather in the world, an act for which I claim neither a longing nor accomplishment—no more than one takes pride in the ability to blink. All I've ever done is as a flicking of the tail, sizing up the feint of every purpose or intent—more generously thought intent—only after I've identified its aftermath, while acknowledging each effort is discerned by this ingenuous economy of results. Am I ever any more than the incipient deficiency of such thinking? Am I—*have* I—any other pith to speak of, to speak through, to tell as though to take...any other than this lavish genealogy of privations? There is nothing more to it, to it or for it, to tell or to take, I have never been more, and I have never been it nonetheless...

φ

Still there comes a time for some fell sword to rend the veil that serves to bind this addled seity within its cambric pale, pushing past the levee of the ego to commence what never realizes its terminal sufficiency as real—as either terminal *or* sufficient, in its order or its frame. Instead another dissolute volition moves to act its lumpen semaphore out loud, signing in another language, with the same gestures, deciphered by a modulation one can never guess. The problem that has led me to this derelict entreaty, I should say, to say as though to tell, to move as though to take, and so to tithe...I can't know how I've been compelled to succor this continuance—this *story*; all others appear so generic by the measure I'm left without a singular distinction to constrain me to the choice, denied the fancy-free alterity of anything but some noetic dispensation of the form of forms...

φ

Any limit deemed an ending can't be held completed...can never *end* for the addition of its own pernicious suffix, and with it I emerge again, the word of the flesh, as the saying never says, a scrivener left with only nail for pen, and only pocked periphery of lard and skin for page. If I could think it all some other way, I trust I would not cower from the view...could climb atop that lissome heap and have the sense it signifies as some fey stillness at the bottom of a stagnant pool, then I would recapitulate the fawning substitution from which I have arisen—from which I *then arose*—and give each thing its name and speak the tell...and hear the substance of the world *as such* in the names of things and their predicates in turn, never to conceive of likeness as identity again...

φ

If I'd done something else I would have found the same I have...if I'd escaped that certainty, to think it all another way by some demurring fallacy, I would not care what means to test the fatuous deceit; could I somehow think it otherwise—embody the *as such* of any such at all—then so I would be, so I would have been, so I would still seem... That it has never happened is beside the point; that I have tried to make it so, to make anything of anything at all, that is, and failed...I have always foundered in that fold, a genius by consistency if nothing else, always lost my way at just the same decisive point, by just the same method; anyone more suited to such consummate awareness might count it auspicious to have happened on this half-caste testimonial, this testament of the half-caste, for the cursory rendition of an obverse...Yes, I say again, I will proceed with what I've started as my method to inscribe the middle passage, and be done with it only at the next beginning, to find myself alone upon that pinhole island of indelible commencements, pulling from all things each thing, and calling each by its own name...

V

Still I can do nothing other than I have, or only as I have, which may amount to nothing, equal in its way to any other absence...I can only do the nothing that I have, and never nothing more, or always nothing, the same difference, each the same, identical but for the dreamed trajectory of discernment. I steer about this harbor by my rudder of a tail, and fixed afore the chevron wake of mantle it propels, I slip through the effrontery of vapors as though it were a reservoir of turgid, glopping gel. The motion is slow, but still abandoned, as the timorous temerity of a pigeon tempted from its fluxing legion by the hint of scattered crumbs, a plumose iridescence thrusting forward with a fealty only as sincere as it is long...

$$\varphi$$

I'm certain I was somewhere, that I was somewhere sometime; perhaps I still am, it's difficult to say. Perhaps I ought to glance about again, to look upon the scape that seeds my gait upon the plain, and find what there...and find what there...And find what there *I find*, by affecting the transcendence of a formerly insensible avoidance, as an eye that attempts to glimpse the back of its head by turning in its socket. I think I'm still enshrined in such a place, if one can call it that, can speak of something, anything at all, as place not incidental to its placement...without, that is, some incident of placement *set within it*, though what this posture might suggest—what impassive bearing the privation of all bearings might *presume*—I don't know, or don't know *if* I know, the same difference, each the same...

φ

I am that place and placement—*every* placement—all the while, I am the place that every placement presently acquires, without which no such stasis could reliably abide. The difficulty of the question—of the *asking* of the question—is nothing to the answer; no puzzlement that's worth the designation can be solved by merely thinking up some ostentatious edict or insidious decline. The *conceit* is difficult to demonstrate, let alone forgo, all in the name of some serenely tacit eavesdropper, whose presence is as though the presence of an absence, thereby contrived as level to the measure of the previous dismissal. It is nothing I am not, or it is only as I'm not if I'm not any other it at all, and I may be, despite all inclinations to the contrary, I may well be indeed...

φ

But that's not quite the proper state or stroke of phraseology; I am never forged in deed, that is, but only in the word that such a deed doth promise is this voluble disposal as the only deed I am, the only I am only as and only if I'm not, and here...I should be here the *what* I am if only there endures no here without me. I am placed...I was placed here, by measure to imagine some procession of exclusions leading into this most postern *locus solus* of bereavements. So again to elocute the situating vision I still siphon through the vizard of an Eleatic bale—I have never seen the place without the placement, not any one at all, and if I think I've come to rest within such fickle thrall, then this, yes, this affirmation only, will lead me from the wallows of that welcoming embrace into...

φ

The pretermitted positure that ties this cinching brigand's noose; the rank infinitesimal, in whose eye I spit my servitude and scrub the greasy image of its filtering translucence...it matters little to the difference I abjure with every glancing grimace and refrain. I have always longed to strap myself to some demersal fin, the back side of a diver's bell careening through the fathoms of a plummetless abyss, but even so I can't desist from casting my descent over the derelict horizon. I might range about this billet and think I've found a wall in one direction or the next, I fall for the trick every time it comes upon me, from the back...and always from the back the mawkish parody descends; I wheel about again to try to catch the tapping stranger, as if to sternward glance had such attention thus been hallowed, but there I find the tip of mordant tail has turned the corner and...I am chasing my own tail, and always that, and nothing...

φ

Who cares that I've been fixed in my position all the while, to find myself at somewhere other than the nowhere I have hitherto beguiled, and having been found there by yet another...by any other anywhere at all, can no longer think it constitutes a novel pose or sector. *I* don't, that is to say, but for the fact that in determining I'm somewhere or other—another somewhere—I have replaced place with placement, and on those grounds alone think to exceed the inhibitions of this resonant enclosure, to exchange the appetitive delights of the voluptuary—the dunderhead of all such facile heroes and heroics—for a peripatetic ease of stride and stratagem. I present the benefactor of this serial without the expectation of acceptance or response, at least not by the evidence presented as its preface; the ruthless vanity of which I may be reasonably accused by such intrepid guild as those who've gathered to perceive it presents as neither sickness or deceit...

φ

It could not...*does* not matter if the description suits or not; any might conceive themselves as some more worthy dimwit for the purpose of this sort of unrepentant hagiography, but they would be mistaken. The estimation of the inestimable can only mock what it has thought esteemed, an appeal to the verisimilitude of a redundancy precisely as cogent as it is superfluous—one is always somewhere, someplace, somehow, regardless of the differential positure one dreams. I appear to have been placed and so to stand within a placement, but as soon as I take stock of the propinquity that such a taking stock inherently construes, it appears to slither back behind the head in whose possession I had thought the declamation at its limit. Each door is an imagined fourth, and any other bound discerned by treading madly through the surf will in the end require one surrender to the flux, whose tidal spew I rush to swallow by the cipher of that visionary excess; every egress dissipates before this fade remorse, while I still long to languish in the den I thought would course to fill that absence...

φ

By all rights it is as...it is *where* I ought to be; such plebeian privilege is never grasped or granted one whose whipping tail is charged with the judicious execution of the plebiscite. One might take it for a rule, or understand it could at least endure the test that any designation of such rulership contrives, but it's only meant to stand as an intransigent aside, and by this lame disclosure I will leave it in the foss that every sidelong highwayman must follow to abide—that somewhere far off and without regard what follows as a following appears the shrill afflatus of some desultory god, and so endears to reportage what otherwise would stand for nothing more than a defiantly capricious goad. I know that in this way my retrograde abandon presents as an appeal to some somatic solecism, I know I lie beside each guileless distention of the senses through the dimming skies, but I don't get it somehow, can't comprehend the limit that I press against without a blush or bruise to signify the fault. I am here, I am there, I was here or there—I find nothing to distinguish one discretion from the next, nothing but what occupies as I do, just and only as I do. The matter of it then is still the only all that matters in the least, as no scope can extend but for the filling of the absence with some equally incontinent rapport, equal to the symbol of the symbol...

φ

All that all the reportage of all such reportage reports, every that this vessel will imprison for conviction—convicted of conviction—is left to ponder the same ordinal conundrum on the way to this result—that no place is conceivable beyond the pith and purview of what radiates as placement set within it. The discernment of each harborage requires somewhere extant other than it is...other than it ever was—

than any ever *were*—a volume only measured by the quantum of its contents, such contents having neither substance nor distinction prior to arrangement in that radix of a matrix—in that carcassed fringe. Such difficulty is only as obvious as it is confounding, a standard of measure by which the acumen of all who think to follow this peculiar supplication can be equally apprized, as every crudely arrogating architect of detectives proffers nothing more than this same resolute perversity for a plenary disguise...

φ

Is it not always the way—the way of all possessed of any way at all—that the difference between following a course still worth the trouble of such vigor once its finished and one's never having done as much as fallen forward towards that end appears a dispensation from the outside only given the dissembling bewilderment of one whose humble query turns that crank upon its mark, as the unremitting circuit of a pump that pumps itself. Nothing worth knowing or worth having been known, nothing apprehended from the seat of such a transcendental throne, can be conceived as anything...*by* anything but this piddling demesne—the quizzical vicissitudes of contra-indication, better set to paradox the second time around...

φ

What use is such extrinsic approbation to this inherent...this *visceral* design? To dismally endorse the dismissal of one dismal claim after another without the need to clamber through its works for a more assured defense, and so sustain a sensual contrivance otherwise unfit to undergo defilement for the incongruity of its physiognomy on paper. A quaint aside, a brief recess before the final assault...It's hard to speak of anything and not nothing—not the nothing that this depredation follows to its end. I can't assert with confidence that I can tell the difference, or how I might yet go about distinguishing the figurement defined by this apportioning of tangents, given, that is, that I don't know what caprice will bring me—and so the heedless pretense of the hero of this *récit*—to a conclusion, mine and ours alike...

φ

Mustn't I have some idea of where I'll stand when I concede I've finished if I'm to claim with any sensible conviction...any *sensibility* at all I haven't yet alighted on that train? Mustn't I know where I've been is not the only where I'll be if I'm to differentiate between such sullen progress—the rhythmic sput and stutter of this lurch into the distance—and the stance I'll stand when I've achieved the advent of its finish? And so it is accomplished by the getting there alone; how else could such portent reach the hand or eye of its maker. It is a stupid claim, adduced by still another voiceless interregnum of ellipses; if it designates a claim in any sense at all it's so much less than any means by which it can enthrall its froward mouthpiece to forestall...

φ

It may seem to you a serviceable phrasing of the point—the point that I am nothing for thinking that I'm nothing, and only something more for thinking that I'm thinking that I'm nothing, and so on. The insight has significance—it *signifies*, that is—what still presents as distant from the shuttle of this roguish annotation, resolving each next query into so much restless mockery, an exegesis taken as sufficient for implying a necessity without median or standard—a necessity discerned by the indulgence of a schema neither sufficient nor necessary for never being both at once. I say again—mustn't I know where I've been to know where I am now, to recognize I'm here and not there, in any other place at all? Mustn't I have already imagined where I'll be when this interpolation meets me where I was if I'm to think I'm moving towards the bourne of an inexorable confinement? All to indicate I'm somewhere, that the space I am, and thus the space I'm *in*, is in itself distinct from that which fills it—an *in* itself that *of* itself is not in at all...

φ

The vessel of creation can only be thought empty if it never is...it never was...and what that fills that vacuum is conceived as other than its placement only if it isn't, if it must be placed no matter what its movement or stagnation in the void. This aggregate totality may seem an empty trope—a tropism as likely—but that inutility does nothing to subtract from its fecundity; so the reservoir of everything interred within the buzzing and translucent ether—of each that must contain the viscid edge of every that's contained—extends only as far as the beginning of such border, contriving the abatement of the substance set within it and equally the *in it* every *in it* in it is...But I get away from myself...*outpace* myself—well, not precisely either. I move further *into* myself, and that field has remained fallow for so long, I'm sure no crop can root without some further tilling of its soil. I may have only simple ox and plough, but it will do, it will do, with the indulgence of any who would take me at my word, it will do quite well indeed...

φ

But...and...well...what a bother; I thought I might extend the metaphor, with ox and field and weed and chaff, all the picaresque piquancy that marks the popular portrait of the hayseed's luckless peril, but it's too much, even for me, even I can't manage to maintain such florid flights of fancy; I suppose I could go back and cut it out entirely—as merciless with the pen as with the lance—but what difference would it make, as though I have no greater purpose than the pandering some impenitent and scrupulous excision would enact, if not require from the moment that the impulse is deduced; in all of it...*for* all of it I can't suggest I ever would do otherwise, or that I ever have done...I never have done otherwise—have always taken back whatever I have taken back already—and any more conspicuous analysis of mistakes and miscues I've committed on my path I put upon the unseen fourth, a *seizure*, as it were, that I can't hope to seize by any other means...

φ

I will wait to tease out any further figure from this pitch and plaster causerie, to take up the consideration by employing the same method it considers, thus to indicate—to *promise*—I will soon continue with it, it will come up anew, but for now I am drawn into...drawn *back*

85

into—as though that in were out again—the selfless disquisition that has brought me to this end, this end and this beginning...If I do not do as I say I do or as I say I will, if I deign to break the pledge by which I've made my way this far, always only this far, it will still guarantee the coming on of that to which the promise appertains by having done the opposite. I am readily made comfortable with such inviolable commitments, and by my supple drollery outwit all who think it as their hostelry to best me by such wits alone. Of other tactics, I don't know; there are certain advantages...but no. Even this will only happen by the same silent decree, accepting I continue towards my culmination by continuing to promise I will culminate—to assert I have concluded—as a shepherd who believes that just beyond the next horizon endures water and green meadow, though never having ventured over that far ridge...

φ

I am here, of this I'm certain; any other capable of self-reflection could make the claim as truthfully, and for this reason the statement is trivial by both nature and implication. Where here *is*—this is the distinction...the *representation* that concerns me, or us, if that's not evident, though as yet the possibility presents no reference of the kind, a kindness offered equally without intent...I won't again surrender a remonstrance to the plaint, the indiscretion of this seemingly refractory caprice having just occurred to me. I know there's something left behind, that the tail holds firm by stretching thin the least conspicuous of narrative ligatures, and so the snapping of that tendon on the Plimsoll line soon promises the measure of a rank I've otherwise forgotten, a place for country and for duty, affixed beneath the churning main of portent and contrition I have always been a martyr to, to or for, the same *I* stricken down...

φ

Such obscure depictions are alone construed by lateral appeals to similarly indeterminate generalizations, and thereby put off any recollection of the state from which I cede this bland and dispossessed arrangement of rights and privileges, as though I were made certain of my membership—my *enrollment*—by my certainty I've failed to yet discern it. The fallacy of the conditional always follows the verisimilitude of that to which the conditional refers—something to ponder as you while away your passage from the harbor to the barren deep. I have only ever given voice to insights likewise privileged into penitent retort for the sake of such crude purposes revealed—for the purposes, that is, of no other rhetorical practice or intent. I am still here, an exception as worthy of this most hastened rendering, for reasons that as likely—and as well—remain unsaid. I am still here, but there is nothing else...

φ

Every state of thingness seems a whisper without person, the model echolalia of some chattering clairvoyant brooding across the centuries, as cogent as the conch shell hiss that dreams the distant sonance of the sea. Each corroborating copula focusses this forlorn synchronicity of qualia, of predicates absented from the orbit of the prime, fringing a container never measurably present till it saturates with portents, a surfeit thought unthinkable outside the shattered weal it circumscribes; filling something, fit to somewhere...It ought to be no problem, then, to show that if I'm anywhere I must also be somewhere, the somewhere every there presumes by centering the idiom of predicates within it. The difficulty is of another order, an order long abstracted from its ordering in turn; who cares, in the end, precisely where I am, where I was, where I will be, if I'm always in the middle, if I'm always on my way to somewhere *else*? It means nothing to describe what I can't seem to stop describing, unless that same description has at first...at *once* evoked the banefully Romantic cadger of some animus unbounded by the supple amphigory, and it hasn't, I say again, the *bête noir* of this chronicle has never been—can never *be*—distinguished from its hero...

φ

What difference where I find myself when such a blinding vagrancy defenestrates the long elided framing of the view, the view of field or mount or sea, whatever blithe transparency will clip past the persistency of every earthly mew? I myself care as an exercise—an exercise *in caring*—and nothing more. That someone *else* might think a setting or a theme will soon bear down upon this bricolage, the *deus ex pudenda* of this prophylactic ward—well then, let them go about their own peculiar business *without* care. The engineer is the dream...Pshaw; what pretense, what ill-considered and irrelevant allusion, although the justification of this censure by the dismissal of its object seems ridiculous to me now. I could as easily expunge the reference, as I've already established, but I don't know which is worse...but it would *certainly* be worse, that is, to allow each odd suggestion of the kind to go unnoticed than it's ever been to hazard disingenuous divergence into literary guise. I refuse to traffic in some narrative profusion by the next reproving shibboleth of esoteric doggerel; I refuse, at least, if it does not suit my fancy to do otherwise, and it does not, a defense that can't *not* constitute this knowingly inconsonant concern...

♀

I am here, yes, I am here. It is enough, though towards what end this proposed sufficiency may lead I cannot...*will* not ever say. The imposture of the fourth wall—that ethereal gudgeon towards which I've addressed this mad encyclical, and which I here submit for the second and last time as though envisioning its ruin—is nothing before the enumeration that precedes it...can only *serve*, that is, as a distraction from the iteration of its precedents. The first who shuttle through the ever proximal substratum, awaiting their hour of victory while holding their breath and clinging to the ground; who slip abaft to catch the turning frontward unawares, remain just that—abaft precisely for each rigorous attempt to bring them round to front again, as though they had been caught within that reticule of causatives before...

♀

Accession to the pacifying rhythm of this puerile *bacchanalia* could never really prod me into action in the least; I want again to ambush what lies in wait behind me, as though one could be pressed against the front of one's own face. It may be I will never find another resolution, or even just a moment's chance to stop and catch my breath, in order to solicit the *next* next before the last has been provided with the terminal exigency of what has long since finished, now no more than swaddled in the dust. And so I think of nothing else, I void my hidebound cask of every other seeming purport...every purport as a purpose...I turn around, and there...and there that there is here...and even here...even here...

φ

Even here there is no landscape. Having long imagined that most disorienting of sublime adventures, I found my stupor stranded on this dissipating strand, lost in the prance of ululating waves, the shoreless shore before me clapping and sighing, sighing and wheezing with the bantam susurrations of each newborn tidal wash. Rightly speaking I have never seen an ocean, nor have I expressed by my reflections the noisome ramblings of the salt sea air, but never still...or *ever*, rather, ever still wouldst one such I think it obliging to require just this tone of melancholy conquest, without an obligation to pursue it. The imperious advent of the mood disorder the quotidian paranoiac more deftly calls a conscience—my first and last submission to the withered caste of a guileless autonomy, a boorish revelation as an I unto myself—excited me to scratch my way over the velum of the seas as but a calming figment, neither willful nor insincere, but without extenuating referent...

φ

Would that such austerity could have languished undisclosed, then now I might...but no. I have neither seen the sea nor stood upon its margins; I have ridden not the thrum of surf by bodice or by sail, despite assertions of my bold and storied exploits at the mercy of the masted gird. And while I have intended no deception by indulging the assurances and reversals of this aspiring sham, nor to rest beneath the canopy of a meager disgust, I have done just that, have I, and so it serves this purpose to have carried such a skillfully disinterested prolepsis only as far as I have, balanced on the shoulders of a grazing lamb. It's not the killing that enchants the artful hunter in the end, for whom the last abasement of the beast presents as a surrendering of pleasure...

φ

How preposterous, if without humor. I believe it's fair to say that on previous remarks I have injured no one so much as myself, and that with little consequence. What harm could there be—what *sort* of harm, even—in the brief, if overwhelming, self-delusion? It's not as if the mask I wear as the featureless visage of a narrative voice adheres to my skull like a second skin, accepting I could know if it did...if it had...that I could readily ascend into the vantage of that second to determine if there'd ever been a first. As long as the verse continues to disport with a supplicating euphony, I don't see how the vocation of the humble dabbler could cease to be awakened, the fierce onslaught of our hero always one step closer to a dispassionate suicide...

φ

And could there be a greater hope for one and all alike, for anyone whose thought-path ambles forward towards a berth cut from the drape of this dissembled transubstantiation? Such declamatory practices may imply a reckless con, but even so I'm solaced by the ambiguity of the referent inured therein—a response aroused as much by my own perversity as by any more momentous exaltation. I feel the stomach rumble, a pressure mounting on the viscera, and know that any further improvisation on the form of the rhetorical will most certainly result in an ending perhaps more competent, but far less entertaining than has ever been my way or wont to prove. Even the loftiest of cerebrations—the most systematic *epoché*—can't help but to surrender to the fleeting borborygmus on its course...

φ

How odd that I thought myself seaward, or seaworthy that I could have been seaward. For the vacuity of that shifting plain, with only the occasional and inadvertent spout to break the line of the horizon, could never keep me...*have kept me* from the wandering and perfervid airs that characterize my manner equally on land. Even here there is no landscape. And so induced to furtive thrush upon the phrenic swells, the warp of elemental causes sheathes the shiftless contours of the whelming shapes beneath, bulging one against another, folding each into the next, and my fleeting acquiescence to some novel phenotype remains distinct in all but substance; the pathos wrought by every idle craning of the neck, attempting to catch the distant and anomalous composure of the world, is neither selfless nor revealing, confirming the intractable inadequacy of the seer. There is a patch of sky that lies within each dank of rot, and a seeping slick of ink shines sometimes more intensely than the blinding break of day...

φ

Being that I am—or being *as* it, in my way—I stake my claim upon no streaky provenance or sterile preterition; every form surrenders to a likeness that is neither *soon-to-be* nor *since-recalled*, but only is—is only *ever* is—and thereby indicates the surplus of its passage into reference. All by way of explanation, suggesting that some earnest apologia might more properly suit such purposes revealed, if yet to administer the promised entertainments of a swashbuckler's memoir. What an impetuous child I must seem, and all for the inaugural misconception of the course of the following—the *reading*—wherein any furtherance of this jovial narration should not pursue the loose tub in its fraying stays, but only the fast fish here singularly designated by its passenger. Better suited, one might think, to the loose than the fast, but for now the labored reference deserves no further scrutiny...

φ

For even up until this turgid present—so the present must appear to those who think to limn it, as the intumescent umbrage of its future passage, curdled into preterit—I have begun the third as an indulgence of the same deception under which the first and second also ran, although in neither, just as now, did the feverish pursuit of the mariner's life prove anything but futile. The indiscretion intimates the question, or rather, the identification of the indiscretion inti-

91

mates the question that the indiscretion hides; that the confession of a surreptitious forgery might be just as worthy of recanting—of *disrepute*—as any besotted narration of events fixed within an actuarial *roman à clef.* Do I not tell the story of the telling by revealing the perversity of the told? And by so doing could one possibly lead the impenitent arbiters of this vicious retinue down the dips and swallows of a long forgotten garden's spastic furrows, a labyrinth fashioned by such negligence alone? If anyone may be so led, are they not more likely to have led themselves? Mine is the history of a lie and then...the restoration—the *recovery*—of something other than that. Which is not to suggest that a fraudulent summation has ever really been exacted by this doggedly naive encomium; it is only a deceit by way of a referent it isn't; it is never false, that is to say, by reference to the referent it is—a principle as true of any other narrative compliance...

φ

What muffled muse can radiate from this unflinching lassitude, what word rest on the squirming tongue corralled in moteless moue; what distance names an interval with end but no beginning, what fitful wind can guide a ship with neither mast nor crew; what meter can recount its own dissevering repose without retiring anew, before I wake with a start from the site of my last interruption, a scattering of berths only granted the safe harbor of its comprehensive scansion insofar as it remains devoid of any buoyant commorant or seaward aperçu. It is all too much to even try again, let alone attempt the next contrivance of an end; I know too much to languish in this paragon of seity without at least a nod to what it's lacking—some assay of all possible divergences along this soon inexpiable course. It is *difficult* enough, I say, to transport this assemblage into something like a chronicle—this endless lore of what will come to seem as without form—as though it were the ever-present yesterday of yesterdays...as though, that is, this world-weary parousia could have ever happened otherwise, but such a hazard pales before the imminence of its betrayal, the putative effacement of all possible effacements...

φ

And who am I to bribe this tail from its retreat in cambric pail, to sink beneath the limpid sail I stutter from the breach? Better to ask what bail I haunt than how I've come upon it, better to know what world is lost than what it's next replacement, by this vocative redress to dress the seas with some broad meaning, to seize the novel crest as though a canopy of stone and rest beneath the fluid armor of that manufactured ceiling. Not I, that is, would be anon inclined to test the shifting lees against the fractured vessel of the lacerated welkin, but passing through the passive voice of that decamping prison can at last adduce the blandishing alterity of feeling, sighted from the anabatic void that I precede; thou shalt see my back parts, my tail, but my face shall not be seen. But I cannot completely make out my back parts; and if I know not even the tail of this whale, how understand its head? Much more, how comprehend its face, when face it has none? Better to wallow in the midden of the shine than to pursue its adumbration, better to return to what has brought me to this line than to follow the next arduous release into the distance. The tenebrae contrived to show the pleasure of the passage is itself the only ending that presents a measure of it, the only eye contrived to glimpse what languishes behind...

φ

To execrate the borders of that cloistered *mare clausum*, to live within the phylum of each next allineation as though it were the rudder of all possible momentum...I have not merely mapped the pressing wide and stormy ocean over the composure of this immotile passion, but finding no terrain on which to make my landing I assign this floss of breakers the innominate elision of a home, at last and first, a home. It is a singular commitment, and one that unconceals no single palliating mode, but both once and again returns the question it refuses, an ever faceless portrait of the portrait it defaces, blotting out all prospect of return to life on shore. Memory is taken back and given by the ocean, but the exile from land can't hazard waver into focus, or maunder into closure, into vantage, into view; gleaners, such as you

and I, are alone enjoined to make a survey of the wreckage, and fash-
ion what remains into...

Glossary

accouchement (*uh*-**koosh**-m*uh*nt; Old French, a-, *to* + coucher, *to lay down*) : the process of giving birth; confinement for said purpose

afflatus (*uh*-**fley**-t*uh*s; Latin, from the verb *afflare*, from *ad*- 'to' + *flare* 'to blow') 1. inspiration; an impelling mental force acting from within 2. divine communication of knowledge

alterity (awl-**ter**-i-tee; Late Latin, *alteritās*, otherness) : the quality or state of being different, or perceived as different

amour propre (a-moor-**praw**-pr*uh*; French) : a sense of one's own worth; self-respect.

amphigory (**am**-fi-gawr-ee; French, *amphigouri*) 1. a nonsense verse or composition 2. a rigmarole with apparent meaning which proves to be meaningless

anamnesis (an am **nee**-sis; Greek, anamnēsis, from *anamimnēskein*, anamnē-, to remind : ana + mimnēskein, *to recall*) 1. recollection or remembrance of past events; reminiscence 2. In *Plato*, deductive recollection of eternal and costitutive ideas 3. a patient's medical history

anomic (an-**uh**-mic; from Greek *anomiā*, lawlessness) 1. Socially unstable, alienated, and disorganized 2. A socially unstable, alienated person

apologia (ap-*uh*-**loh**-jee-*uh*; Greek, a verbal defence, from apo- + *logos* speech) 1. a formal defense or justification, of a belief, idea, etc 2. a work written as an explanation or justification of one's motives, convictions, or acts

appanage (**ap**-*uh*-nij; Old French, *apaner*, to make provisions for) : something (as a property or perquisite) claimed as rightful to some position or rank; a grant of said by sovereign or governing apparatus

auto-da-fé (aw-toh-d*uh*-**fey**; Portuguese auto da fé : *auto*, act + *da*, of the + *fé*, faith) 1. Public announcement of the sentences imposed by the Inquisition 2. Public execution, especially by burning at the stake

avulse (*uh*-**vuhls**; Latin āvellere, to tear off) : to pull off or tear away forcibly

banderole (**ban**-d*uh*-rohl; Italian *banderuola*, small banner) 1. a small flag or streamer fastened to a lance or masthead 2. a narrow scroll bearing an inscription

battology (b*uh*-**tol**-*uh*-jee; Greek *battología*, stammerer) : futile or wearisome repetition in speech or writing

Bildungsroman (**bil**-d*oo*ngz-roh-mahn; German : *Bildung*, formation + *Roman*, novel) : a narrative principally focussed on the education, development, and maturing of a young protagonist

billet-doux (**bil**-ey-**doo**; French : *billet*, short note + *doux*, sweet) : a love letter

borborygmus (bawr-b*uh*-**rig**-m*uh*s; Greek *borborugmos*, of imitative origin) : rumbling of the stomach

bricolage (bree-k*uh*-**lahzh**; French, from *bricole*, trifle, from Old French, catapult) 1. a construction from materials at hand; something created from a variety of things 2. a piece of makeshift handiwork

bromide (**broh**-mahyd; from use of some bromides as sedatives) : a commonplace or hackneyed statement, notion, or person

brumous (**broom**-uhs; Latin *hrūma*, winter) : foggy, misty

bulwark (**buhl**-werk; Middle Dutch *bolwerc*, from *bolle*, tree trunk + *werc*, work) 1. a structure raised as a defensive fortification; a rampart 2. something serving as a bulwark; a defense or safeguard

carapace (**kar**-*uh*-peys; from Spanish *carapacho*): a protective, shell-like covering

caudal (**kawd**-l; from Latin *cauda*, tail) 1. of, at, or near the tail or hind parts; posterior: *the caudal fin of a fish.* 2. Situated beneath or on the underside; inferior 3. Similar to a tail in form or function

causatum (**kawz**-at-*uh*m; Latin, effect) : something that is caused; an effect

causerie (**koh**-*zuh*-ree; French, *causer*, to talk) 1. an informal discussion or chat, especially of an intellectual nature. 2. a short conversational piece of writing or criticism

Charybdis (k*uh*-**rib**-dis; from Greek): a whirlpool off the Sicilian coast, opposite the cave of Scylla

circumbendibus (sur-k*uh* m-**ben**-d*uh*-b*uh*s; coined from Latin *circum* round about + English *bend* + Latin *-ibus*, ablative ending) : an indirect or circuitous course especially in writing or speaking; circumlocution

conatus (koh-**ney**-t*uh*s; Latin, effort) 1. an effort or striving derived from natural impulse 2. a force or tendency simulating effort 3. in Spinoza, the force in every animate creature to persist in its own being

consecution (kon-si-**kyoo**-sh*uh*n; Latin *cōnsecūtiō*, orderly sequence) 1. sequence or succession 2. relation of consequent to antecedent; deduction

corselet (**kawrs**-lit; diminutive of Old French *cors*, body) : body armor, especially a breastplate; cuirass

crapulence (**krap**-y*uh*- l*uh* nts; from Late Latin *crāpulentus*, very drunk) 1. sickness caused by excessive eating or
drinking 2. excessive indulgence; intemperance

decussate (**dek**-*uh*-seyt; from *decussis*, the number ten, from the Romans' use of X for the numeral 10) : to cross in the form of an X; intersect

deliquesce (del-i-**kwes**; Latin, *de-* + *liquēscere*, to melt) : 1. to become liquid by absorbing moisture from the air 2. to melt away 3. to form many small divisions or branches.

defenestrate (dee-fen-*uh*-streyt; Latin, *de-* + *fenestra*, window) : to throw out of a window

desiccate (**des**-i-keyt; Latin, *siccus*, dry) 1. to dry thoroughly; dry up 2. to become thoroughly dried or dried up

deus ex pudenda (**dey**-*uh*s eks pyoo-**den**-d*uh*; Latin *deus*, god + *ex*, from + *pudenda*, the shameful; genitalia) : back formation from *deus ex machina*

diacritical (dahy-*uh*-**krit**-i-k*uh*l; Greek *diakrīnein*, to distinguish) 1. marking a distinction 2. able to discriminate or distinguish 3. serving as a diacritic

diametric (dahy-*uh*-**me**-trik; Greek *diametrik(ós)*, diameter) 1. of, relating to, or along a diameter
2. exactly opposite; contrary

dight (dahyt; Old English *dihtan*, dictate, appoint, ordain) : outfit, as verb or noun

distrait (dih-**streyt**; French, *distraire*, to distract) : inattentive or preoccupied, especially because of anxiety; absent-mnded

echolalia (ek-oh-**ley**-lee-*uh*; Latin, from echo + Greek *lalia*, talk, chatter) 1. the uncontrollable and immediate repetition of words spoken by another person 2. the imitation by a baby of the vocal sounds produced by others

eidos (**ahy**-dos; Greek, form) 1. an abstraction belonging to or characteristic of an entity 2. in Aristotle, the active, determining principle of a thing as distinguished from its matter 3. in Husserl, what a thing is in its invariable and essential structure, apart from all that is contingent to it 4. the formal content of a culture, encompassing its system of ideas, criteria for interpreting experience

Eleatic (el-ee-**at**-ik; Greek, place name Elea) : relating to a school of philosophy founded in Elea in Greece in the 6th century BCE by Xenophanes, Parmenides, and Zeno, which held that one pure immutable Being is the only object of knowledge and that information obtained by the senses is illusory

encomium (en-**koh**-mee-*uh*m; Greek *enkōmion*, (speech) praising a victor) : warm glowing speech; a formal expression of praise

entelechy (en-**tel**-*uh*-kee; Greek *entelēs*, complete) 1. a realization or actuality as opposed to a potentiality 2. a vital agent or force directing growth towards self-fulfillment

epoché (e-poh-**kee**; Greek, suspension): the state where all judgments about non-evident matters are suspended; in Husserlian phenomenology, a process involved in blocking biases and assumptions in order to explain a phenomenon in terms of its own inherent system of meaning

eschaton (**eska**-ton; Greek *eskhatos*, last) : the final event in the divine plan; the end of the world

etiology (ee-tee-**ol**-*uh*-jee; Greek *aitiā*, cause) : any study of cause, origination, or causality

foss (fos; Latin, *fossa* terra, dug earth) : a ditch, trench, moat, or canal

ganglia (**gang**-glee-*uh*; Latin pl of *ganglion*, tumor, swelling) 1. a mass of nerve tissue existing outside the central nervous system 2. any of certain masses of gray matter in the brain, as the basal ganglia 3. a center of intellectual or industrial force, activity

glossolalia (glos-*uh*-**ley**-lee-*uh*; Greek *glōssa*, tongue, language): incomprehensible speech, often associated with a trance state, or an episode of religious ecstasy

golem (**goh**-l*uh*m; Hebrew, shapeless mass, embryo) : in Jewish folklore, a figure constructed in the form of a human being and animated by hermetic means

Guignol (gee-**nyawl**; from *Le Grand Guignol*, a theater in Paris) : of, relating to, or being a short drama emphasizing horror and gore

Gordian (**gawr**-dee-*uh*n; Greek) : complex to the point incomprehensibility; resembling the Gordian knot in intricacy

gramary (**gram**-*uh*-ree; French *grimoire*, incantation) : occult learning; magic

heuristic (hyoo-**ris**-tik; Greek *heuriskein*, to find) 1. serving to indicate or point out; stimulating interest as a means 2. of furthering investigation of, relating to, or based on experimentation, evaluation, or trial-and-error methods

hic et nunc et ubique (**heek** et **nuhngk** et **oo**-bee-kwe; Latin) : here and now and everywhere

Histoire Extraordinaire (French, extraordinary history; amazing story) a collection of short stories by Edgar Allen Poe translated and collected under this title by Baudelaire

illation (ih-**ley**-shuhn; Latin *illātiō*, act of bringing in) 1. the act of inferring or drawing conclusions 2. a conclusion drawn; a deduction

imposthume (im-**pos**-chyoom; Greek, *apostēma*; separation of pus) : a collection of pus or purulent matter in any part of an animal body; an abscess

ineluctable (in-i-**luhk**-tuh-buhl; Latin *inēluctābilis*, impenetrable) : not to be avoided or escaped; inevitable

integument (in-**teg**-yuh-muhnt; Latin *integere*, to cover over) 1. a natural covering, as a skin, shell, or rind 2. any covering, coating, or enclosure

interregnum (in-ter-**reg**-nuhm; Latin, between reigns) 1. an interval of time between the close of one sovereign's reign and the accession of a successor 2. any period of freedom from the usual authority 3. any gap or interruption in continuity.

introit (**in**-troh-it; Latin, *introitus*; a going in, an entering, entrance) : a choral response sung at the beginning of a religious service

innominate (ih-**nom**-uh-nit; Latin *nominatus*, to name) : having no name; nameless; anonymous

lapidary (**lap**-i-der-ee; Latin *lapidarius*, stonecutter) 1. of or relating to the cutting or engraving of precious stones 2. characterized by an exactitude and extreme refinement that suggests gem cutting

"a lickerous mouth moste han a lickerous tayl" Geoffrey Chaucer, Prologue of the Wyves Tale of Bath

locus solus (**loh**-k*uh*s **soh**-l*uh*s; Latin) : solitary or unique place; a work by Raymond Rousel, published 1914.

Lorelei (**lawr**-*uh*-lahy; German) : a legendary nymph on the river Rhine who lured sailors to wreck on the rocks by singing

lustrate (**luhs**-treyt; Latin *lustrare*, to purify) : to purify by propitiatory offering or other ceremonial method.

lusus naturae (**loo**-s*uh*s n*uh*-**toor**-ee; Latin) : freak of nature; mutant

Ister (**is**-ter; place name) : the Greek name for the Danube river; see *Der Ister*, Friedrich Hölderlin

marl (mahrl; Latin *marga*, marl) : a friable mixture of clay and other minerals; earth

mare clausum (**mah**-re -**klou**-s*oo*m; Latin, closed sea) : a body of navigable water under the sole jurisdiction of a nation or other authority

mephitic (m*uh*-**fit**-ik; Latin *mephitis*, noxious vapor, especially from the earth) : noxious; pestilential; poisonous

mountebank (**moun**-t*uh*-bangk; Italian *monta im banco*, one gets up onto the bench) 1. a person hawker of quack medicines in public places, attracting an audience by tricks, storytelling, and jokes 2. a flamboyant charlatan or quack

noesis/noetic (noh-**ee**-sis/noh-**et**-ik; Greek, *noein* to perceive) 1. the functioning of the intellect; understanding occurring through direct knowledge, i.e., solely through the intellect 2. in Husserl, the subjective aspect of or the act in an intentional experience—distinguished from

noema 3. in Plato, the highest knowledge, of the eternal forms or ideas—contrasted with *dianoia*

nous (noos; Greek, mind) 1. an intelligent purposive principle of the world; in Stoicism, the Logos 2. the rational part of the individual human soul; reason and knowledge as opposed to sense perception 3. in Neoplatonism, the first emanation of the divine, equal to divine reason and containing the cosmos of intelligible beings

oblation (o-**bley**-sh*uh*n; Latin *oblatus*, to offer) : the act of making an offering, especially to a deity

ontic (**on**-tik; Greek *onto*, being) : relating to or having real being

ontogeny (on-**toj**-*uh*-nee; Greek *onto*- + -*geny*, being + genesis) : the development or developmental history of an individual organism.

opprobrium (*uh*-**proh**-bree-*uh*m; Latin, *opprobrāre*, to reproach) 1. something that brings disgrace 2. contempt, reproach

palimpsest (**pal**-imp-sest; Greek *palimpsestos*, scraped again) 1. a parchment from which writing has been erased and overwritten 2. something that has a new layer, aspect, or appearance that builds on its past and allows us to see or perceive parts of this past

parastasis (**pahr**-ah-**stey**-sis; Greek) : the relationship among causal mechanisms that can compensate for, or mask defects in, each other

paratypic (**par**-*uh*-tip-ik; Greek) : diverging from type

parlous (**pahr**-l*uh*s; perilous; Greek *peira*, trial) : perilous; dangerous.

Parousia (p*uh*-**roo**-zee-*uh*; Greek *parousia*, presence) 1. (Plato) the presence in any thing of the idea after which it was formed 2. (Christianity) the second coming

peripatetic (per-*uh*-p*uh*-**tet**-ik; Greek *peripatētikos*, given to walking about) 1. walking or traveling about; itinerant 2. of or relating to Aristotle, who taught while walking in the Lyceum

persiflage (**pur**-s*uh*-flahzh; French, *persifler*, to banter) 1. frivolous banter 2. frivolity or mockery in discussing a subject

phrenic (**fren**-ik; Greek *phrēn*, the diaphragm) 1. relating to the mind or mental activity 2. of or relating to the diaphragm

phronesis (froh-**nee**-sis; Greek) : in Aristotle, the practical wisdom that allows for the social and political pursuit of ethical imperatives; both necessary to and sufficient for being virtuous

philippic (fi-**lip**-ik; after the orations of Demosthenes against Philip of Macecon) : a bitter attack or denunciation; invective

pleonasm (**plee**-*uh*-naz-*uh*m; Greek *pleonasmos*, more than enough) 1. the use of more words than are necessary to express an idea; redundancy 2. a redundant word or expression

poesis (poh-**ee**-sis, Greek *poēsis*, composition, poetry) 1. the process of making; production, creation; creativity, culture 2. poem; poems collectively, poetry, verse; poesy

praxis (**prak**-sis; Greek, *prāssein*, to do) 1. exercise or practice of an art, science, or skill 2. customary practice or conduct

pretermit (pree-ter-**mit**; Latin *praetermittere*, let pass, overlook) 1. to let pass without notice; disregard 2. to leave undone; neglect; omit 3. to suspend or interrupt

priapic (prahy-**ap**-ik; Greek *Priapos*, son of Dionysus and Aphrodite, personifying male reproductive power) 1. of or relating to Priapus; phallic 2. suggestive of or resembling a phallus by its shape 3. exaggeratedly concerned with masculinity and male sexuality

prolepsis (proh-**lep**-sis; Greek, *prolambanein*, to anticipate) : the representation or assumption of a future act or development as if presently existing or accomplished

propinquity (proh-**ping**-kwi-tee; Latin *propinquitatem*, nearness, vicinity) 1. nearness in place; proximity 2. nearness of relation; kinship 3. affinity of nature; similarity 4. nearness in time

quadrate (**kwod**-reyt; Latin *quadratum*, square, squared) : to cause to conform or harmonize; adapt

qualia (**kwah**-lee-*uh*; Latin *qualitatem*, a quality, property) 1. qualities regarded as independent objects 2. sense data or feelings having a distinctive quality

quiddity (**kwid**-i-tee; Latin *quidditas*, the essence of things) 1. the quality that makes a thing what it is; the essential nature of a thing 2. a trifling nicety of subtle distinction, as in argument

quotidian (kwoh-**tid**-ee-*uh*n; Latin *quotidianus*, daily) : usual or customary; everyday

radix (**rey**-diks; Latin, root) : a root or point of origin

revanche (r*uh*-**vanch**; French, revenge) : the act of retaliating, especially by a nation or group to regain lost territory or standing; revenge

revenant (**rev**-*uh*-n*uh*nt; French *revenir*, to return) : one who returns after death or long absence

rictus (**rik**-t*uh*s; Latin *ringī*, to gape) : a gaping grimace

roman à clef (raw-mah na-**kle**; French, novel with a key) : a narrative involving historical events and characters under the guise of fiction

sacerdotal (sas-er-**doht**-l; Latin *sacerdotalis*, of or pertaining to a priest) : of priests; priestly

sans gêne (sahn-**zhen**; French) without constraint or embarrassment; free and easy

shibboleth (**shib**-*uh*-lith; Hebrew, from the use of this word in Judges 12:6 as a test to distinguish Gileadites from Ephraimites (the latter pronouncing the word as 'sibboleth') resulting in the slaughter of 42,000 Ephramaites) 1. a word or pronunciation that distinguishes people of one group or class from those of another 2. a custom or practice that betrays one as an outsider

skein (skeyn; Irish *sgainne*, a coil, clue) 1. anything wound in or resembling a coil 2. a succession or series of similar or interrelated things

solecism (**sol**-*uh*-siz-*uh*m; Greek *soloikos*, speaking incorrectly) 1. a non-standard or ungrammatical usage 2. a breach of good manners or etiquette 3. any error, impropriety, or inconsistency

sophism (**sof**-iz-*uh*m; Greek *sophisma*; clever device, stage-trick) : any false argument; fallacy

soutane (soo-**tahn**; Latin *subtus*, beneath) : a cassock

Stygian (**stij**-ee-*uh*n; Greek *Stygios*) 3. of or relating to the river Styx or to Hades 2. dark or gloomy 3. infernal; hellish

subitaneous (suhb-i-**tey**-nee-*uh*s; Latin, sudden) : formed or taking place suddenly or unexpectedly

succedaneum (suhk-si-**dey**-nee-*uh*m; Latin *succēdere*, to succeed) : a substitute

suzerain (**soo**-*zuh*-reyn; French, from adverb *sus*, up, above, on analogy of *souverain*) 1. a sovereign or a state exercising political control over a dependent state 2. a feudal overlord

synecdoche (si-**nek**-d*uh*-kee; Greek, a receiving together or jointly) : a figure of speech in which a part is used for the whole or the whole for a part, the special for the general or the general for the special

taxon (**tak**-son; Greek *taxis*, arrangement) : a taxonomic category, as a species or genus

teratoid (**ter**-*uh*-toid; Greek *teratos*, a monster) : resembling a monster

terminus ad quem (**tur**-m*uh*-n*uh*s ad **kwem**; Latin, limit to which) : a goal, object, or course of action

tropism (**troh**-piz *uh*m; from Greek *tropos*, turn, figure of speech) : movement of an organism in the direction of a stimulus, such as light or gravity, especially by growth

tropology (troh-**pol**-*uh*-jee; from Greek *tropos*, turn, figure of speech) 1. the use of figurative language in speech or writing 2. a treatise on figures of speech or tropes 3. the use of a Scriptural text so as to give it a moral interpretation or significance apart from its direct meaning

vatic (**vat**-ik; Latin *vates*, sooth-sayer) : of, relating to, or characteristic of a prophet

villous (**vil**-*uh*s; Latin *villus*, shaggy hair) : covered with long soft hairs

volte-face (volt-**fahs**; Italian *voltafaccia*) : a reversal in policy; about-face

voluptuary (v*uh*-**luhp**-choo-er-ee; Latin *voluptārius*, devoted to pleasure) 1. a person devoted or addicted to luxury and sensual pleasures 2. of, relating to, characterized by, or furthering sensual gratification or luxury

welkin (**wel**-kin; Old English *wolcen*, cloud) : the sky; the vault of heaven

whorl (hwurl; Middle English *whorle*) 1. anything shaped like a coil 2. one of the central ridges of a fingerprint, forming at least one complete circle

Steven Seidenberg's other works include *plain sight* (Roof Books | 2020), *Situ* (Black Sun Lit | 2018), *Null Set* (Spooky Actions Books | 2015), and *Itch* (RAW aRT Press | 2013). He is also the author of the photomonographs *Pipevalve: Berlin* (Lodima | 2017) and *The Architecture of Silence: Abandoned Lives of the Italian South* (Contrasto | 2022).

Anon
Steven Seidenberg

Cover image from the series "Rome Squares," by Steven Seidenberg

Cover typefaces and interior typeface: Garamond Premier Pro

Cover and interior design by Ken Keegan

Printed in the United States
by Books International, Dulles, Virginia
On 55# Glatfelter B19 Antique 360 ppi
Acid Free Archival Quality Recycled Paper

Publication of this book was made possible in part by gifts from
Katherine & John Gravendyk in honor of Hillary Gravendyk,
Francesca Bell, Mary Mackey, and The New Place Fund

Omnidawn Publishing
Oakland, California
Staff and Volunteers, Spring 2022

Rusty Morrison & Ken Keegan, senior editors & co-publishers
Laura Joakimson, production editor and poetry & fiction editor
Rob Hendricks, editor for *Omniverse* & fiction, & post-pub marketing,
Sharon Zetter, poetry editor & book designer
Liza Flum, poetry editor
Matthew Bowie, poetry editor
Anthony Cody, poetry editor
Jason Bayani, poetry editor
Gail Aronson, fiction editor
Jennifer Metsker, marketing assistant